No One Left Standing

Other Books on Testing from Rowman & Littlefield

Zarra, E. J. (2015). *The Wrong Direction for Today's Schools: The Impact of Common Core on American Education.*
Lucido, H. B. (2015). *Returning Sanity to the Classroom: Eliminating the Testing Mania.*
Durham, G. (2014). *Standardized Testing Skills: Strategies, Techniques, Activities to Help Raise Students' Scores (Second Edition).*
Schneider, S. (2013). *How Parents Can Help Kids Improve Test Scores; Taking the Stakes Out of Literacy Testing (Second Edition).*
Wurdinger, S. D. (2011). *Time for Action: Stop Teaching to the Test and Start Teaching Skills.*
Hursh, D. (2008). *High-Stakes Testing and the Decline of Teaching and Learning: The Real Crisis in Education.*
Johnson, D., Johnson, B., Farenga, S., and Ness, D. (2007). *Stop High-Stakes Testing: An Appeal to America's Conscience.*
Vairo, P. D., Marcus, S., and Weiner, M. (2007). *Hot-Button Issues for Teachers; What Every Educator Needs to Know about Leadership, Testing, Textbooks, Vouchers, and More.*
Schneider, S. (2006). *How Parents Can Help Kids Improve Test Scores: Taking the Stakes Out of Literacy Testing.*
Hanshaw, L. G. (2006). *Cooperative Classroom Testing.*
Johnson, D. D., and Johnson, B. (2005). *High Stakes: Poverty, Testing, and Failure in American Schools (Second Edition).*
Jones, G. M., Jones, B. D., and Hargrove, T. (2003). *The Unintended Consequences of High-Stakes Testing.*
Elford, G. W. (2002). *Beyond Standardized Testing: Better Information for School Accountability and Management.*

No One Left Standing

Will the Rewrite of NCLB Be Enough?

Michele Wages

ROWMAN & LITTLEFIELD
Lanham • Boulder • New York • London

Published by Rowman & Littlefield
A wholly owned subsidiary of The Rowman & Littlefield Publishing Group, Inc.
4501 Forbes Boulevard, Suite 200, Lanham, Maryland 20706
www.rowman.com

Unit A, Whitacre Mews, 26-34 Stannary Street, London SE11 4AB

Copyright © 2017 by Michele Wages

All rights reserved. No part of this book may be reproduced in any form or by any electronic or mechanical means, including information storage and retrieval systems, without written permission from the publisher, except by a reviewer who may quote passages in a review.

British Library Cataloguing in Publication Information Available

Library of Congress Cataloging-in-Publication Data
Names: Wages, Michele, 1965- author.
Title: No one left standing : will the rewrite of NCLB be enough? / Michele Wages.
Description: Lanham : Rowman & Littlefield, [2016] | Includes bibliographical references.
Identifiers: LCCN 2016018987| ISBN 9781475822625 (cloth : alk. paper) | ISBN 9781475822632 (pbk. : alk. paper) | ISBN 9781475822649 (Electronic)
Subjects: LCSH: Educational tests and measurements—United States. | Education—Standards—United States. | United States. No Child Left Behind Act of 2001.
Classification: LCC LB3051 .W256 2016 | DDC 371.260973–dc23
LC record available at https://lccn.loc.gov/2016018987

∞™ The paper used in this publication meets the minimum requirements of American National Standard for Information Sciences—Permanence of Paper for Printed Library Materials, ANSI/NISO Z39.48-1992.

Printed in the United States of America

Contents

Foreword		vii
Preface		xi
Introduction		xv
1	Why Experts Say We Need Standardized Tests	1
2	Why Teachers Say We Don't Need So Much Testing	9
3	What's Wrong with Standardized Tests?	15
4	So Why Do We Test?	25
5	The Other Costs of Standardized Tests	31
6	How Is the Increase in Child Poverty Affecting Standardized Testing?	37
7	How Is the Increase in Cultural Diversity Affecting Standardized Testing?	43
8	What Do Standardized Tests Actually Reflect?	49
9	Are There Benefits to Standardized Testing?	55
10	Are There Alternatives to Standardized Testing?	61
11	Will the Reauthorization of the Elementary and Secondary Act Fix the Problems?	67
Conclusion		77
References		79
About the Author		87

Foreword

How Should You Select a Book about Educational Tests?

Every teacher will tell you a test is not a measure of what a kid knows.
—Teacher Darcy White, quoted by Rojas and Rich, 2015

Every teacher collects books about education. Novice teachers rely on them extensively. If novice teachers could have only five books for their collections, what topics would they choose?

The beginner teachers would have an easy time with the first three books. They would make sure that they had at least one book on instruction, another on curriculum, and still another on classroom management.

For their fourth book, these teachers would have to deliberate carefully. They would have to select it from a wide range of topics. Some of them would choose a book on school technology. Others would focus on student diversity. Still others would choose one on learning materials.

For their fifth book, the novice teachers would have to be even more cautious. After all, this would be their last book! They would want to be sure that it represented a topic that would be critically important to them. They might be so nervous that they would go to senior colleagues for advice.

The beginner teachers might be surprised by the advice that they received from the experienced teachers. Although they would not receive the same recommendation from every one of them, they certainly would get one recommendation more than any other.

The novice teachers would be advised to make sure that they had a book about educational testing.

* * *

Once the beginner teachers resolved to select a book about educational testing, they would have to check about the materials that were available to them. They might go to a retail website, such as Amazon.com. Then they could investigate the number of educational testing books that were listed on it. Should they use this approach, they would discover an inventory of over 28,000 books on this single topic.

If they think that the Amazon inventory might be mistakenly inflated, they could check on the educational testing books that were cataloged within libraries around the world. They might go to a professional website such as WorldCat.org. Should they use this approach, they would encounter an inventory of over 200,000 books on this topic.

The novice teachers, like many experienced teachers, would be overwhelmed by the abundance of materials on educational assessment. How could they possibly select the optimal book?

The beginner teachers already would have an intuitive sense of the type of book that they would value. They would want one that was interesting, objective, clearly written, practical, and sensitive to reputable scholastic practices.

We can surmise the traits that these teachers would value when they were searching for a book on educational assessment. Are those traits different from those that senior teachers, school counselors, school administrators, superintendents, school board members, policy makers, and parents would value?

All of these groups might wonder if Michele Wages' book—*No One Left Standing: Will the Rewrite of NCLB Be Enough?*—has any of the characteristics that they prized.

* * *

No One Left Standing is genuinely interesting. Readers will be engrossed by the quotes at the beginnings of the chapters. As just one example, they will be struck by a quote by Michelle Obama: "If my future were determined just by my performance on a standardized test, I wouldn't be here."

No One Left Standing is remarkably objective. It highlights the many features of learning that cannot be measured by tests but that profoundly influence children in school. Nonetheless, it never calls for an end to tests. It instead suggests ways that the disadvantageous features of tests can be restricted and the benefits of them maximized.

No One Left Standing is clearly written. The chapters begin with common-sense discussions of contentious assessment issues. They then amplify those discussions with examples. Finally, they conclude with suggestions about how contentious issues can be resolved.

No One Left Standing is practical. It suggests ways to modify tests, accompany them with complementary measures of student performance, replace them with more accurate measures of teacher performance, and constrain the influence that politicians and businesspersons have on them.

No One Left Standing is sensitive to reputable scholastic practices. It bolsters key points with citations from researchers, teachers, and professional educational organizations.

This book will be treasured by teachers, school counselors, school administrators, superintendents, school board members, policy makers, and parents. It will appeal to them because it is interesting, objective, clearly written, thoroughly researched, and extraordinarily practical.

Gerard Giordano, Ph.D.
Professor of Education
University of North Florida

REFERENCE

Rojas, R. and Rich, M. (January 27, 2015). States move to make citizenship exams a classroom aid. *New York Times*. Retrieved from: http://www.nytimes.com/2015/01/28/us/states-move-to-make-citizenship-exams-a-classroom-aid.html.

Preface

The Educational Law known as No Child Left Behind (NCLB) was enacted in 2002, and subsequent federal mandates brought about a significant increase in accountability testing by requiring the testing of all students in grades 3–8 and some grades in high school. "The federally mandated tests are used to sanction schools and, in extreme cases, to close some schools or convert them to charter schools" (Nelson, 2013). This law expired in 2007 and until December 2015, had yet to be reauthorized, rewritten, or readdressed.

As the only economically advanced nation to rely heavily on high stakes, standardized, multiple choice tests, the United States has put all its eggs in one basket. "High stakes" can have many meanings depending on one's perspective. For the purposes of this book, it is when a student's educational future is based from a score, whether a teacher's contract will be renewed, or whether penalties will be applied to a school such as removal of professionals or a complete rewrite of the school's approaches. Tests are said to be "standardized" when all students answer the same questions under similar conditions and their responses are scored using the same measurement.

The two main types of standardized tests used in U.S. public schools are:

1. **Aptitude:** Predict how well students are likely to perform in some subsequent educational setting. (Examples: *SAT* is a standardized college entrance test to help colleges and universities identify students who could succeed at their institutions and to connect students with educational opportunities beyond high school. *ACT* is a national college admissions examination that consists of subject area tests in English, mathematics, reading, and science.)
2. **Achievement:** Relied upon by citizens and school board members to evaluate a school's effectiveness. (Examples: *California Achievement Test*, for

grades 2 and 4–12, is a nationally normed standardized test that measures achievement in the areas of reading, language arts, and math. *Iowa Test of Basic Skills* is a national test for K–12 students. It allows the comparison of your child's reading, language arts, math, social studies, and science scores with children across the country. *Stanford Achievement Test* is a set of tests used by school districts in the United States and in American schools abroad for assessing children from kindergarten through high school. *Comprehensive Tests of Basic Skills* is a national test administered to all students in grades 3, 6, and 9 in reading, language, and math. *Metropolitan Achievement Test* is an individually administered test of reading achievement. The length of the test is approximately three hours and covers the content of math, reading, and language. *CogAT* is used to measure verbal, quantitative, nonverbal or spatial symbols, and reasoning and problem-solving skills.)

The reasons given by educational politics as to the need for high-stakes standardized testing are that it provides a valid measurement of the child's achievement and holds teachers accountable for providing quality education to all students. Sounds great! But this is not what is really happening.

As with any assessment that would choose one day out of an entire instructional year to measure a child's mastery, there is no control over how that child is faring emotionally, physically, or psychologically for that short window of time of one day. Drilling students on sample questions for weeks before a state test will not improve their standards either.

But let's also consider the low-income minority groups, English Language Learners (ELLs), and students with disabilities. Because of this one standardized test on day one, they may be denied diplomas, retained, or placed in lower track or remedial education programs for the rest of their entire school experience. This labels them as low achieving and often results in heavy kill and drill activities that ensure they will fall further behind. The rationale? If they can't pass the test, it is because they need more rote drill and test practices.

The truth? According to Kohn (2000), tests that measure as little as multiple-choice exams can neither provide accountability that is meaningful, nor build life skills for students. How many real-life situations have you come across in your lifetime where you were given four choices? "Standardized tests are not based on general knowledge, but on specific knowledge contained in specific sets of books; the textbooks created by the test makers" (Broussard, 2014).

Let's also add that states believe student results on these tests are also a reliable measure of teacher quality. This is equivalent to evaluating a teacher's performance to a "flip of the coin" or a "roll of the die." No wonder so many fabulously talented educators are leaving the field or refusing to accept positions at high-poverty schools. The pressure of the results on one day's assessment affects not only their paycheck and job security, but also their value.

This book was written to shed light on not only why we supposedly test our children to death under the outdated NCLB and continuing with the Every Student Succeeds Act but also who profits from it, which may be the reason the law had been left expired for eight years. In addition, it also includes the rewrites voted into law allowing you to determine if it will really rebuild the damage that has been done in America's public schools.

Introduction

Every public school student in the United States will experience various types of testing every year. For decades, the purpose and quality of such testing, the time it takes to administer and take the test, and how the data is used are the topics of discussion among students, parents, educators, and policymakers. Those supporting the importance of testing have a perception that more testing will improve student achievement and seem to be wearing blinders about the additional costs involved. Those against excessive testing believe that schools are sacrificing learning time in order to test or prepare for the test. They also believe that reduced learning time of nontested subjects occurs and more time is given to those students who are performing right below the proficiency score, or "bubble kids," instead of developing every student's full potential.

The 1990s saw an explosion of state-mandated testing beginning with students in select grades being tested once a year to measure school performance in comparison with the "standards." In a study by Hanushek and Raymond (2006), it was concluded that student achievement improved faster in the first states that adopted a standards-based reform when compared to the states that had not implemented testing. Teachers don't mind the idea of higher standards; what they do mind is the fact that end-of-the-year tests are not useful in improving the day-to-day instruction in their classroom.

The NCLB law, enacted in 2002, and subsequent federal mandates brought about a significant increase in accountability testing by requiring the testing of all students in grades 3–8 and some grades in high school. "The federally mandated tests are used to sanction schools and, in extreme cases, to close some schools or convert them to charter schools" (Nelson, 2013).

The creation of the federal Race to the Top (RTTT) program added fuel to high-stakes testing by requiring teacher evaluations to be based in part on student achievement measured by test scores, as well as on other measures not related to testing. Many may not realize that waivers were given by the government in order to sidestep sanctions of NCLB for states that adopted their own test and enacted a teacher evaluation system that resembled their prescriptive criteria. There also exists the federal School Improvement Grant (SIG) program that inevitably threatens schools with conversion to charter schools or closure, and threatens staff with job loss, all based on student performance on these mandated tests.

Many types of assessments are used in U.S. schools. Most are required by the state, while others are chosen or developed at the district level. In addition, it is also the case that almost all of a district's student assessment inventory is linked to federal laws and regulations other than NCLB. In many respects, because of the emphasis on the data that assessment results contain, nearly every assessment has become a high-stakes assessment with attached consequences for students, teachers, and schools.

According to Nelson (2013), the different types of tests used in the majority of public schools include:

Diagnostic Testing. Various assessments are used within and across districts that provide information as to each student's strengths and weaknesses in order for educators to adjust curriculum and instruction so that they can differentiate to meet students' needs. Other assessments measure basic literacy skills, while still others are given to all students in the early grades but only to struggling students in subsequent grades.

College Entrance Exams and Advanced Placement. Many college-bound students find themselves wanting to take advanced placement or International Baccalaureate courses that also include national tests.

Classroom-Based Assessments. These assessments are used during teaching and are embedded in instruction; they are a tool that helps teachers adjust their instruction in the moment to meet the needs of students. Now this isn't just referring to giving a quiz at the end of class, it includes those informal assessments teachers give by asking questions and making observations of student performance on specific tasks. Using these assessments allows teachers to use the immediate results in order to adjust their instruction in a timely manner. Teachers also use tests, quizzes, and homework to assess student learning. "Teachers surveyed in Chicago spent twenty-two minutes a day giving students curriculum subject assessments (tests, quizzes, etc.) and another thirty-two minutes a day assessing students' work during contractual hours" (Bruno, Ashby, and Manzo, 2012).

Embedded and Rapid Assessments. Embedded assessments could be thought of as the "next-generation" formative assessment. "Assessments embedded in instructional materials using emerging technology and research on learning aims to inform instruction through a balance of fine-grained classroom diagnostic tests, challenging tasks and projects in which students work through individual topics at their own pace, taking brief tests of their mastery along the way, with feedback delivered to the student and teacher on individual processes or misconceptions that cause the student problems" (Gordon Commission, 2013).

State-Mandated Summative Tests. These are designed to assess whether students are meeting state standards in a given year. In most cases, the tests are given in the spring and are looked upon as a means of "summing up" what students know that year, which is why these tests are referred to as summative assessments. The results of these tests are tied to the state's accountability system as mandated by NCLB. When linked to prior-year summative test scores, student progress can be measured, which provides some information about how well schools or teachers did in the current testing year, the true measure of school effectiveness. Unfortunately, today's reality includes a single summative test taken by students across the United States which supposedly measures student achievement to enable state and federal governments to sanction districts. A student's actual growth and progress is not measured just by how they compare to the norm and therefore cannot show a school's contribution to learning over the year.

Interim/Benchmarking Assessments. Interim or benchmark assessments are often given by districts in addition to the standardized tests. These interim tests are given in order to measure student growth toward passing the year-end mandated test (Heppen et al., 2011). Benchmark assessment results are ultimately available throughout the school year in order to identify where targeted instructional interventions are needed to reteach low-scoring concepts and group students for tutoring. This is not the case for state-mandated summative assessments.

A survey of curriculum coordinators and research directors revealed that "while nearly all respondents believed that the purpose of interim assessments was to guide and improve instruction, 90 percent of the same respondents believed they measure progress toward the end-of-year state test, 80 percent believed they were also diagnostic and 90 percent thought they were formative" (Heppen et al., 2011).

Testing in U.S. public schools is out of control. In most cases, the effects of stress and pressure related to the testing process cannot even be measured. Is this really the best thing for our schools? Are there alternative measures that may serve our future in a better way?

Chapter 1

Why Experts Say We Need Standardized Tests

If my future were determined just by my performance on a standardized test, I wouldn't be here. I guarantee you that.

—Michelle Obama

Norm-referenced and group-administered tests are the most prevalent tests given in schools today. These have been very widely used for many decades. It is also common that the results are used to evaluate a student's achievement and inform as to what skills need to be learned and determine the school's effectiveness in teaching these skills. The results can also help parents and teachers understand their child's strengths and weaknesses throughout different content areas (Association of Test Publishers [ATP], 2014).

Although high-quality assessments generate rich data that provides valuable information, supports accountability, and promotes high expectations, they were designed to encourage equity for students of color and low-income students through the No Child Left Behind Act of 2001. In reality, however, this kind of test simply collects information. Its effectiveness lies in the quality of information collected and the way the information is utilized.

When high-quality assessments are correctly used, they can be an invaluable tool for teachers and parents in determining areas in which students struggle, how they are progressing, and where the educational gaps lie. The data from these assessments can also assure policy makers and advocates that students are receiving a high-quality education (Lazarin, 2014).

According to Supovitz (2015), there are four major theories that underlie our current reliance on high-stakes tests:

- The first is *motivational theory*. This is based on the idea that the accountability of the test will motivate improvement in the student's achievement.

It is the predominant theory underlying test-based accountability. This concept is also based on the belief that teachers' performance is motivated by the extrinsic rewards and sanctions that are attached to high-stakes testing.

However, the belief that the more external pressure a teacher receives, the more improved their teaching becomes the truth is that the majority of educators already have a strong internal sense of responsibility, which is why they chose the profession as a career. This reason skews the research, making it inconclusive about the actual effects of external pressure. To defend this, there are as many researchers who have found that reward does not decrease intrinsic motivation (Cameron and Pierce, 1994), and those who have concluded that tangible rewards often undermine internal motivations (Deci et al., 1999).

- The second is the *theory of alignment*, which is just as it sounds, in that in the test accountability there will be more concerns with making sure that the major components of the test become components of the educational system itself. For example, if the standards, curriculum, and assessments are aligned through district or educator efforts, then they will reinforce each other and become more effective, while also improving the system as a whole.

"Alignment is usually thought of in terms of synchronizing the surrounding system, but can also be thought of as alignment between the external accountability of schools and schools' sense of internal accountability" (Supovitz, 2015).

- The third theory is *information theory*, which is also much like you would imagine in that through the data and information gained from the testing, improvement in various areas can be guided. *Information theory* takes the stance that educators should use the high-stakes performance data in order to make decisions about programs and curriculum as well as guiding what happens in both the classroom and the organization as a whole.
- The last theory is *symbolism*, in other words, with the spotlight on the high-stakes testing, a system signal, or symbol, is created to the stakeholders reinforcing its importance and value. *Symbolism theory* is a model in which the accountability system provides the public the right to expect that their tax dollars are being used responsibly. By reporting high-stakes test scores, evidence is provided that the public education system is making rigorous academic efforts in the caretaking of the students.

THE PROS OF STANDARDIZED TESTING

Based on Kemmerling (2005), the pros of standardized testing are discussed in this section.

The scores can be compared to those of other students within the same school or across schools and districts. These scores can identify not only the abilities of the individual student but also the strengths and weaknesses of the campus easily.

Because standardized tests provide a longitudinal report of student progress, educators are able to track growth and find pattern trends that aid in responding to students' educational needs in a more timely manner.

The data provided by standardized tests helps improve prediction and selection for gifted programs, colleges, scholarships, or employment. Achievement and ability tests can also be used as a reliable predictor for college success.

The results of the testing can provide feedback to students about their own knowledge, which associates the students' personal efforts to their skill levels, which, in turn, motivates them to work harder in school.

The tests help teachers to work more effectively because the data allows them to identify areas of strengths and weaknesses in their instruction and promotes restructuring lessons. The data from the tests will help teachers to also identify what content was not mastered by students and see which students have the greatest need. This information will encourage teachers to be more motivated to participate in professional development and support services to improve their instruction.

The relationships between teachers and teachers as well as teachers and students evolve through standardized testing. This creates greater cohesion among teachers and promotes collaboration and an openness to new ideas. For today's schools to be effective, a link between teacher performance and student learning is essential.

By revising the district curriculum and testing programs to become consistent with state curricula, accountability is provided at the school level, which betters the chances of positive changes occurring. Another positive effect is that it often leads districts and schools to use their resources more effectively, such as hiring more qualified teachers, and providing tutoring sessions after school. Results from standardized tests can also help reallocate funds to schools that performed well and deserve a reward or to those schools most in need.

The bottom line is that the greatest problem with U.S. schools isn't high dropout rates or underqualified teachers but standardized testing. Nationwide newspapers are replete with articles about the push being made by parents and teachers in Buffalo, Philadelphia, Seattle, and elsewhere to help students opt out of taking standardized tests. One major reason is that the parents feel that their children are being taught to pass a test instead of the skills needed to be productive adult citizens.

According to economist Dan Ariely of Duke University, the dilemma is that many believe that it is within this method that improvement can be maximized. He goes on to state that in the business world, "CEOs care about stock value because that's how we measure them. If we want to change what they care about, we should change what we measure" (Ariely as stated by Augustine, 2013). Can this be transferred to education in which you are dealing with people, however, and not a business?

In an article by Concordia University (2015), the arguments in favor of standardized testing include the following:

Accountability to Stakeholders

These tests provide data to taxpayers that informs them of how students and teachers are performing.

Measure of Achievement for College Readiness

For many students, setting themselves apart from others in their high school is difficult. Tests like the SAT and ACT provide students the hope, even if their schools have limited advanced placement courses, that they still have the potential to be successful in college. The down side affects those students who attend schools with substantial enrollment or are highly competitive where it is harder for them to stand out among the pool of highly qualified students. Making it to the top 10 percent of the class in this environment can affect students' self-esteem and motivation regardless of the talent they have.

Consistent Assessment

As in most professions, each person processes information differently. In today's classroom, one cannot ignore the fact that every teacher grades differently, and has different expectations used for evaluation. As you can imagine, this factor can also impact how admission committees evaluate and prioritize the importance of a student's overall GPA. With standardized testing data, the scales become a bit more balanced by providing colleges with relatively objective data that can be consistently compared to that of other prospective students.

Teacher Evaluation

Over the past few years, several states have implemented an appraisal system that ties student performance to teacher evaluations. The National Council on Teacher Quality (2014) reported that "about a third of all states had adopted evaluation policies requiring teacher evaluations to include objective measures of student achievement as a significant or preponderant criterion in teacher evaluations."

This report also noted that these teacher policy grade reforms have been attributed to a full grade-level improvement in the areas of teacher evaluation and effectiveness.

Yet, according to Goldhaber (2002), this is not the case. In their study, it was found that only

> 8.5 percent of the variation in student achievement was due to teacher characteristics and the vast majority (60 percent) of differences in student test scores were due to individual and family background characteristics. All the influences of a school, including school-, teacher-, and class-level variables, both measurable and immeasurable, were found to account for approximately 21 percent of the variation in student achievement. This 21 percent is composed mainly of characteristics that were not directly quantified in the analyses. (Goldhaber, 2002)

Yet another analysis by Rivkin, Hanushek, and Kain (2005) for the Center for Public Education states that the following teacher qualities are related to higher student achievement:

- **Content knowledge:** Effective teachers have a college major or minor in the subject area they are teaching.
- **Teaching experience:** They have a minimum of five years of teaching experience. This supports other research in which teacher inexperience can result in greater obstacles in student achievement (Center for Public Education, 2005).
- **Teacher training and credentials:** There has always been a dilemma about whether certified teachers are more effective than uncertified, or alternatively certified, particularly in the content area of mathematics. Research suggests that in general, those with emergency certificates have not resulted in as high of performance rates as those with a traditional certification. But there are conflicting opinions about teachers from the Teach for America (TFA) program who become alternatively certified. In a study by the University of South Florida (2002), it was shown that TFA teachers showed greater gains.
- **Overall academic ability:** Few can dispute that teachers with stronger academic skills perform better in all areas, including SAT and ACT scores, grade-point average, or college selection and scholarships.

In an experiment by The Tennessee Department of Education's STAR project (1985–1990), the effects of smaller classes on student achievement over a period of four years were closely evaluated. Not surprisingly, the data revealed that teachers exercised a substantial influence on student achievement. It was also discovered that if students had high-quality teachers over a period of their schooling, greater gains were made in their learning than those who had less effective teachers one after another.

Findings from the University of Texas-Dallas Schools Project supported the findings from the Tennessee study. In their analysis of the data, Rivkin, Hanushek, and Kain (2005) found that "teacher quality differences explained the largest portion of the variation in student reading and math performance of Texas students in grades K–12 from 1990–2002."

The evidence collection in the Tennessee and Texas studies showed that teachers make a substantial difference in student achievement. Unfortunately, neither defines the characteristics of an "effective teacher." One must sift through other research to help pinpoint the specific attributes of teacher quality (Goe and Stickler, 2008).

In the case of new teachers, performance and outcome data is not yet available, making it necessary to use a teacher's qualifications to regulate entry into the classroom. Collecting data about a teacher's qualifications is cost-effective and relatively easy and may also be used as indicators of teacher quality. The question, however, remains: Are a teacher's qualifications also an effective criterion of identifying teachers who contribute to their students' achievements?

Goe (2007) discerned the following two-key teacher qualification variables that, across studies, are consistently shown to produce strong, positive effects on student learning:

- **Teachers' knowledge of subject matter:** This affects the students at all school levels, particularly at the secondary level. One example is in the area of mathematics, in which it appears that teachers with stronger mathematical skills and knowledge produce better student achievement in mathematics compared with less knowledgeable teachers.
- **Teachers' level of experience:** In the teaching profession, the first five years are the most crucial. It is during these years that teachers either gain in their skills to contribute to student learning or get totally disillusioned and frustrated and quit the profession. It is unfortunate, however, that once the first five years are over, this contribution of experience to student learning appears to level off.

These results clarify that each of these measures shows a positive relationship to student performance, but these same studies also vary in their assessment of how strong an effect each dimension has on student outcomes. A better predictor of student performance is the actual knowledge teachers have about the subject matter they are teaching. In the world of education, the representation of one's content knowledge is usually measured by one's college degree.

If a teacher has a degree with a minor in field. Darling-Hammond (1999) found that "although other factors had a stronger association with achievement, the presence of a teacher who did not have at least a minor in the subject matter that he or she taught accounted for about 20 percent of the variation in NAEP scores."

If a teacher has a major in field. Goldhaber and Brewer (1997) found that the "presence of teachers with at least a major in their subject area was the most reliable predictor of student achievement scores in math and science." They also concluded that "an advanced degree that was specific to the subject being taught was accountable for higher student achievement versus those without an advanced degree." There is also contradictory research in this area. Some studies found that graduate level training in a specific content area did not produce higher performing students (Rivkin, Hanushek, and Kain, 2005; Ferguson and Ladd, 1996).

As you can see, research indicates many viewpoints on what has the largest effect on student achievement. Standardized testing is just one predictor of how successful a student or class will be, yet more headlines, news stories, and debate address testing than any of the others. In today's schools, we must find a balance of all the factors in order to best serve our students.

Chapter 2

Why Teachers Say We Don't Need So Much Testing

I care more about the people my students become than the scores on the tests they take.

—Anonymous

Although innumerable reasons are given against standardized testing, the two most common are well documented. The first is quite simple: tests are just not necessary. The second one takes a stance that most of us are familiar with: the costs associated with tests are just too high when compared to their effectiveness in being a benchmark of basic skills (Jouriles, 2014).

The fact is, most teachers feel standardized tests are unnecessary because, more often than not, they do not show anything that they don't already know. Any teacher who works with kids can tell you which ones can read and write. Letter grades and evaluations that break down progress on particular skills is a much better indicator of a student's achievement than a test given once a year. In other words, trust the teacher.

Today's teachers do not need a test given on one day of the year to tell them what students know. They are professionals who craft assessments in order to make sure they can accurately determine what the students know. These assessments are given constantly throughout the year, both formally and informally, along with reviewing their daily work and behaviors (Clarke, 2015).

Another reason teachers are against standardized tests is that in some years, their classrooms can be filled with difficult students, which will affect variations in test score performance. These differences can sometimes be substantial, and there is no leeway for a teacher when 75 percent of their students are reading two years behind grade level at the beginning of the year. The increasing number of ELLs and special-needs students in today's classrooms can also lower the value of scores (Anrig, 2015).

A third reason for this perspective on testing is that there are hundreds of factors in every classroom that can affect a student's performance, all of which are outside of the teacher's control. A child's experiences at home with siblings or parents, with peers, on their way to school, during breakfast in the cafeteria, can all critically impact how students perform on standardized tests. In a 2011 study whose conclusion was part of a report by the American Education Research Association and the National Academy of Education, the authors wrote: "With respect to value-added measures of student achievement tied to individual teachers, current research says that high-stakes, individual level decisions, or comparisons across highly dissimilar schools or student populations, should be avoided" (Anrig, 2015).

The fact of the matter is that using test scores to judge teachers isn't just ineffective, it is the key reason today's schools are experiencing a teacher shortage. The most highly qualified teacher can have a year of low test scores and thus be given a less than satisfactory evaluation. This can cause a chain reaction, which may include them losing self-confidence in their abilities or, worse, possibly leaving the profession all together. Another example of how the current evaluation system fails is in the fact that it creates an unhealthy competition and perpetuates isolation between teachers, who fear that if they share their strategies and ideas with others, it may skew the bonus pool and actually punish the teacher who shares (Anrig, 2015).

Another reality is that the enrollment in teacher training colleges has been substantially decreasing by between 20 and 50 percent in big states like New York, California, Texas, and North Carolina over the past five years. At the same time, the rate at which teachers are leaving urban school districts is skyrocketing. By states adopting this value-added evaluation and compensation policy, teacher morale has reached its lowest level ever especially in the low-socioeconomic-level urban schools. Teachers want schools that nurture a culture focused on a shared sense of mission, and one where they feel valued and appreciated, in other words, a place they can't wait to get to every day. For in reality, when the teachers have an environment like the one just described, then education is genuinely adding value for the students that attend. Until stakeholders realize that evaluations and scores should not be connected, this pathway to student achievement and job satisfaction will never exist.

In the reality of today's schools, test scores are not being used for the purposes of diagnosing strengths and weaknesses, but as an unfair measure in which to evaluate (and penalize) schools, teachers, and students. Since the bipartisan passage of the NCLB Act in 2002, "Adequate Yearly Progress," or one year's growth in reading and math, has been measured solely on test performance. Failure can result in the student being held back a grade, or retained. Unfortunately the stress that is being placed on the students and the teachers is beyond doubt unreasonable. It does not account for those students who are simply poor test takers or are nonmedicated and have attention deficit disorder (ADD) or are new to the country and English is not their first language. The fact is that as it is now, standardized testing will never be able to capture all the brilliance the youth of our generation has. Some students are great thinkers but horrible testers and vice versa. Real intelligence comes in many forms and it is a dynamic concept (Erickson, 2012).

Another downfall to standardized tests is that oftentimes when a teacher's ability to do a good job is judged upon their students' tests scores, it creates substantial amounts of pressure on them to spend all of their class time teaching students only material that will be on the test. When teachers are forced to aim their main focus on teaching only things that will be on the test, it creates a negative impact on the students because there is so much more they should be learning during that year of school.

The most absurd hallmark of high-stakes testing thus far is the implementation of teacher evaluation systems that assess teachers on the test scores of students they don't have and/or subjects they don't teach. It is a tragedy that it has been in place for so long. The majority of high-stakes standardized tests are given only in math and English language arts, and the data is calculated by mathematical formulas designed to figure out how the art or music teachers who don't teach math and English can be judged by those test scores regardless. "In fact, for a few years in Washington D.C., every adult in every public school building, including custodians and lunchroom workers, were evaluated in part by the school's average test scores. Teachers in some states have sued to stop this practice" (Strauss, 2015).

Specific educators' feedback on the useless data derived from standardized testing includes statements from a long-time gifted and talented teacher. She claims, "We care deeply about student learning, but we don't get any useful information from these tests. By the time scores are reported, those students have moved on. Every group of students is unique, and we can't assume that the next group will have the same needs or abilities. These tests are more a distraction from productive teaching and learning than anything else" (Shell Lockwood as reported by Ravitch, 2015a).

A twenty-eight-year veteran teacher includes his input: "For me, it's a matter of social justice, we might as well pass out scores on the basis of family income. These tests pretend to offer an objective measure of student learning, but really discriminate against students who have parents working multiple jobs, who have limited home resources for activities that support learning, and who may go home to a bare cupboard instead of a warm, nourishing meal" (David Sudmeier as reported by Ravitch, 2015b).

Educators were behind the overwhelming rush to raise standards in schools, and it was not done for educational reasons. Rather, these unrealistic standards were mandated by politicians and corporate executives for political reasons. The unfortunate effects have been to squeeze the intellectual life out of classrooms and create a disproportionately destructive effect on poor and minority kids while also driving out some of our best teachers. Schools have come to resemble test preparation factories.

The majority of the population does not understand the limits of public education. Having only one teacher per twenty (to forty or more) students hugely impacts what teachers can accomplish in the best of systems. The basic theory of education is the Socratic dialogue. Its main purpose is to promote ongoing dialogue and interaction between a teacher and a few students who, in turn, are also encouraged to question and challenge the teacher and then the teacher reciprocates in a back-and-forth interaction. Using this structure, the teacher is able to continually assess the students' understanding of the subject matter on the basis of what those students ask and answer.

The reality of today's classroom setting, however, is that it has become an artificial learning environment where curiosity is squelched by the sterile structure of the curriculum and instruction. This, in addition to the teacher-to-student ratio (I have been in classrooms where teachers have thirty-seven to forty students in core subject areas), squelches the kind of interactive dynamic that makes learning natural and lively. Even the best public school teachers who have managed to find ways to supplement the public school setting have not been able to dissolve the endless limitations. This has resulted in a field day for education "reformers" who are eager to point out the inadequacies and shortcomings when they have a political agenda or an innovation to push. "Testing has always seemed necessary to assess the learning of students whose numbers make it impossible for teachers to know them well enough to measure individually their knowledge of subjects" (Hach, 2014).

Let's face the facts. Although policymakers would like us to believe that the "real purpose" of standardized assessment is to assess student learning, educators know that the true purpose is to rank the students themselves from winners and losers or successes and failures. This derives from the twentieth-century American capitalist viewpoint that there must be enough "losers" at testing to be able to fill the assembly lines of industry as well as unemployment lines. "Unions mitigated this feature of capitalism for a time, to the benefit of all workers, which is why unions have been under assault by the corporate state and now struggle to survive" (Hach, 2014).

In the past, testing was used to identify people of lower intelligence in order to address their deficiencies and return them to the "normal" intelligence pool. In today's society, standardized testing is used as a tool to overwhelm the public school system with an abundance of substandard students, leading them to the likely future of unemployment, imprisonment, and a life most likely lived below the poverty line.

The fact of the matter is that when students regurgitate memorized information, they are unable to process and retain it through understanding.

The skill of memorizing has become a permanent substitute for understanding in today's school system. An example would be a typical spelling test in which a student memorizes the words for a test, but when asked a week later cannot remember how the word is spelled. Students don't purposefully forget the information; their minds reject it simply because human brains are not designed to learn through memorization or through the regurgitation of facts. Understanding is a process that takes time and must be combined with various resources in order to process the information input into knowledge. Without the bridge between information and knowledge, understanding cannot happen.

Those who back standardized testing claim that these assessments do not measure the memorization of information but test students' reading comprehension, composition skills, and math skills on the basis of what the students have been taught and are already supposed to know. The reality is that standardized tests contain text and subject matter of which students have little to no prior knowledge. The result is putting students through a traumatic experience that basically assesses their test-taking skills. When reading is taught, skimming a passage to answer multiple-choice questions is not one of the decoding, comprehension, or phonological strategies, yet that is what it has become in today's classrooms. The same can be said for writing, which has been reduced to a small allotment of time in which to produce a rough draft. The result is a generation of students for whom reading comprehension and writing as the process of drafting, revising, and editing are lost arts.

Unfortunately, public school teachers have been getting the blame, but in reality, they are as much victims of the system as the students. The truth of the matter, as long as standardized tests exist, is that teachers will teach to the test and students will become master test takers. Teachers will continue to want their students to be successful, but when looked at as simply a score on a test, success is devalued and public schools will continue to fail.

Not so long ago students in public schools were taken on field trips in order to provide them with experiences and build prior knowledge of subjects in order to develop reading comprehension through a broad range of subjects. With standardized testing and focus on core standards, these opportunities have been replaced with more curriculum and less real-world experiences. This leaves the responsibility of field trips to fall on to the parents who, with the current economy, must work multiple jobs, more hours, and take on other commitments to survive (Hach, 2014).

Field trips have become an obscure event in today's public schools as funding is redirected to time, resources, and money required for testing. Only when educators and policy makers realize that this money is better spent on real-world activities such as visiting museums, watching plays, or studying plants in the botanical gardens will the students be better equipped with background knowledge and become live participants in their own education.

In reality, we really don't learn much from standardized tests and it is indeed sad that the education system has given them so much prominence. Today's common core standards are doomed to fail because of this accountability and partial reforms which have only disappointed people while standards and testing continue to run their course (Jouriles, 2014).

Could we try one alternative? We could just place our trust in the teachers and schools to report their students' progress, including the tool used to measure the score they have. After all, they are the professionals who are with the students seven hours a day and probably know the students better than many of their parents. "It will avoid a plethora of social, emotional, and political costs. Any bureaucracy created can't be more of a drag on the government or economy than the legion of consultants and think tanks today feeding off the trough of education" (Jouriles, 2014).

Chapter 3

What's Wrong with Standardized Tests?

One of the most distressing characteristics of education reformers is that they are hyper-focused on how students perform, but they ignore how students learn.

—Diane Marie

A nine-year study by the National Research Council (2011) found that measurement experts agree that no test is good enough to serve as the sole primary basis for any important educational decision. The study continued by listing some of the negative consequences, including:

- Narrowing of curriculum.
- Teaching to the test.
- Pushing students out of school.
- Driving teachers out of the profession.
- Undermining student engagement and school climate.
- Exit tests used by twenty-five states determined that high-school graduation disproportionately penalizes low-income, minority, ELL, and disabled students.
- They do not promote the knowledge, skills, and habits needed for success in college or skilled work.
- Retention is almost always academically and emotionally harmful and generally does not lead to sustained academic improvement, lowers self-esteem, and leads to dropping out.

The following are the additional negative impacts according to Strauss (2014):

1. **Lost Learning Time:** Between district benchmark assessments and other tests such as CoGat and TeLPAS, there is less time for learning
2. **Reduced Content Knowledge:** The focus is on high-stakes testing which results in students not being able to demonstrate subject mastery when different formats of testing are used. For instance, if a student has been programmed to choose from four answer choices and then is given a short-answer essay format, they are lost.
3. **Shut Out of Some Programs:** Results can exclude some students from gifted and talented programs or prevent them from enrolling in advanced courses.
4. **Diverted Resources:** Schools that perform poorly sometimes have resources taken away from them.
5. **Loss of Curiosity and the Love of Learning:** Bubble tests are developmentally inappropriate for young learners. Many have problems coloring in the bubbles without going out of the lines, which can skew the computer grading program. But, more importantly, it takes away from the natural curiosity and imagination of these young children and isn't that what we all remember about our early elementary years?
6. **Harmful Stress:** Pressure causes children to throw up, lose control of their bowels, and increase anxiety issues. This can cause them to not want to go to school and leave emotional scars they will carry for a lifetime.
7. **Internalized Failure:** Students who fail believe they are worthless and cannot succeed. This can cause students to drop out or worse, to consider suicide.
8. **School Closures:** When labeled as failing on the basis of test scores, schools can be closed.
9. **Blocked Access to Facilities:** Oftentimes, fine arts programs and computer labs are closed during testing windows as the staff or the room is used to administer tests.
10. **Graduation Requirements:** Some exams force too many children out of school based on a single score.

Still doubt that disadvantages exist? In an article on the use of standardized tests to improve education in America, ProCon (2015) reports the positive and negative aspects of standardized testing on the basis of documented research (see Table 3.1).

Regardless of whether or not you believe the pros and cons list given in Table 3.1, the bottomline is that standardized tests don't provide any feedback on how to perform better. Educators and students are not given the results until months after taking the test and are not provided strategies or

Table 3.1 Pro & Con Arguments: "Is the Use of Standardized Tests Improving Education in America?"

PRO Standardized Tests	CON Standardized Tests
1. **Ninety-three percent of studies on student testing, including the use of large-scale and high-stakes standardized tests, found a "positive effect" on student achievement**, according to a peer-reviewed, 100-year analysis of testing research completed in 2011 by testing scholar Richard P. Phelps.	1. **Standardized testing has not improved student achievement.** After No Child Left Behind (NCLB) passed in 2002, the US slipped from eighteenth in the world in math on the Program for International Student Assessment (PISA) to the thirty-first place in 2009, with a similar drop in science and no change in reading. A May 26, 2011, National Research Council report found no evidence test-based incentive programs are working: "Despite using them for several decades, policymakers and educators do not yet know how to use test-based incentives to consistently generate positive effects on achievement and to improve education."
2. **Standardized tests are reliable and objective measures of student achievement.** Without them, policy makers would have to rely on tests scored by individual schools and teachers who have a vested interest in producing favorable results. Multiple-choice tests, in particular, are graded by machine and therefore are not subject to human subjectivity or bias.	2. **Standardized tests are an unreliable measure of student performance.** A 2001 study published by the Brookings Institution found that 50–80 percent of year-over-year test score improvements were temporary and "caused by fluctuations that had nothing to do with long-term changes in learning . . ."
3. **Twenty school systems that "have achieved significant, sustained, and widespread gains"** on national and international assessments used "proficiency targets for each school" and "frequent, standardized testing to monitor system progress," according to a Nov. 2010 report by McKinsey & Company, a global management consulting firm.	3. **Standardized tests are unfair and discriminatory against non-English speakers and students with special needs.** English-language learners take tests in English before they have mastered the language. Special education students take the same tests as other children, receiving few of the accommodations usually provided to them as part of their Individualized Education Plans (IEP).
4. **Standardized tests are inclusive and nondiscriminatory because they ensure content is equivalent for all students.** Former Washington, DC, schools chancellor Michelle Rhee argues that using alternate tests for minorities or exempting children with disabilities would be unfair to those students: "You can't separate them, and to try to do so creates two, unequal systems, one with accountability and one without it. This is a civil rights issue."	4. **Standardized tests measure only a small portion of what makes education meaningful.** According to late education researcher Gerald W. Bracey, PhD, qualities that standardized tests cannot measure include "creativity, critical thinking, resilience, motivation, persistence, curiosity, endurance, reliability, enthusiasm, empathy, self-awareness, self-discipline, leadership, civic-mindedness, courage, compassion, resourcefulness, sense of beauty, sense of wonder, honesty, integrity."

(Continued)

Table 3.1 Pro & Con Arguments: "Is the Use of Standardized Tests Improving Education in America?" (Continued)

PRO Standardized Tests	CON Standardized Tests
5. **China has a long tradition of standardized testing and leads the world in educational achievement.** China displaced Finland as number one in reading, math, and science when Shanghai debuted on the Program for International Student Assessment (PISA) rankings in 2009. Despite calls for a reduction in standardized testing, China's testing regimen remains firmly in place. Chester E. Finn, Jr., Chairman of the Hoover Institution's Koret Task Force on K-12 Education, predicts that Chinese cities will top the PISA charts for the next several decades.	5. **"Teaching to the test" is replacing good teaching practices with "drill n' kill" rote learning.** A five-year University of Maryland study completed in 2007 found "the pressure teachers were feeling to 'teach to the test'" since NCLB was leading to "declines in teaching higher-order thinking, in the amount of time spent on complex assignments, and in the actual amount of high cognitive content in the curriculum."
6. **"Teaching to the test" can be a good thing because it focuses on essential content and skills, eliminates time-wasting activities that don't produce learning gains, and motivates students to excel.** The US Department of Education stated in Nov. 2004 that "if teachers cover subject matter required by the standards and teach it well, then students will master the material on which they will be tested—and probably much more."	6. **NCLB tests are drastically narrowing the curriculum.** A national 2007 study by the Center on Education Policy reported that since 2001, 44 percent of school districts had reduced the time spent on science, social studies and the arts by an average of 145 minutes per week in order to focus on reading and math. A 2007 survey of 1,250 civics, government, and social studies teachers showed that 75 percent of those teaching current events less often cited standardized tests as the reason.
7. **Standardized tests are not narrowing the curriculum, rather they are focusing on important basic skills all students need to master.** According to a study in the Oct. 28, 2005, issue of the peer-reviewed Education Policy Analysis Archives, teachers in four Minnesota school districts said standardized testing had a positive impact, improving the quality of the curriculum while raising student achievement.	7. **Instruction time is being consumed by monotonous test preparation.** Some schools allocate more than a quarter of the year's instruction to test prep. [Kozol] After New York City's reading and math scores plunged in 2010, many schools imposed extra measures to avoid being shut down, including daily two and a half hour prep sessions and test practice on vacation days. On Sep. 11, 2002, students at Monterey High School in Lubbock, TX, were prevented from discussing the first anniversary of the 2001 terrorist attacks because they were too busy with standardized test preparation.
8. **Increased testing does not force teachers to encourage "drill n' kill" rote learning.** According to a study in the Oct. 28, 2005, issue of the peer-reviewed Education Policy Analysis Archives, good teachers understand that "isolated drills on the types of items expected on the test" are unacceptable, and principals interviewed said "they would not sanction any teacher caught teaching to the test." In any case, research has shown that drilling students does not produce test score gains: "Teaching a curriculum aligned to state standards and using test data as feedback produces higher test scores than an instructional emphasis on memorization and test-taking skills."	8. **Standardized tests are not objective.** A paper published in the Fall 2002 edition of the peer-reviewed Journal of Human Resources stated that scores vary due to subjective decisions made during test design and administration: "Simply changing the relative weight of algebra and geometry in NAEP (the National Assessment of Educational Progress) altered the gap between black and white students."

9. **Most parents approve of standardized tests.** A June-July 2013 Associated Press-NORC Center for Public Affairs Research poll found that 75 percent of parents say standardized tests "are a solid measure of their children's abilities" and 69 percent say the tests "are a good measure of the schools' quality." 93 percent of parents say standardized tests "should be used to identify areas where students need extra help" and 61 percent say their children "take an appropriate number of standardized tests."

10. **Testing is not too stressful for students.** The US Department of Education stated: "Although testing may be stressful for some students, testing is a normal and expected way of assessing what students have learned." A Nov. 2001 University of Arkansas study found that "the vast majority of students do not exhibit stress and have positive attitudes towards standardized testing programs." Young students vomit at their desks for a variety of reasons, but only in rare cases is this the result of testing anxiety.

11. **Most students believe standardized tests are fair.** A June 2006 Public Agenda survey of 1,342 public school students in grades 6–12 found that 71 percent of students think the number of tests they have to take is "about right" and 79 percent believe test questions are fair. The 2002 edition of the survey found that "virtually all students say they take the tests seriously and more than half (56 percent) say they take them very seriously."

12. **Most teachers acknowledge the importance of standardized tests and do not feel their teaching has been compromised.** In a 2009 Scholastic/Gates Foundation survey, 81 percent of US public school teachers said state-required standardized tests were at least "somewhat important" as a measure of students' academic achievement, and 27 percent said they were "very important" or "absolutely essential." A total of 73 percent of teachers surveyed in a Mar. 2002 Public Agenda study said they "have not neglected regular teaching duties for test preparation."

What's Wrong with Standardized Tests? 19

9. **Standardized testing causes severe stress in younger students.** According to education researcher Gregory J. Cizek, anecdotes abound "illustrating how testing . . . produces gripping anxiety in even the brightest students, and makes young children vomit or cry, or both." On Mar. 14, 2002, the Sacramento Bee reported that "test-related jitters, especially among young students, are so common that the Stanford-9 exam comes with instructions on what to do with a test booklet in case a student vomits on it."

10. **Older students do not take NCLB-mandated standardized tests seriously because they do not affect their grades.** An English teacher at New Mexico's Valley High School said in Aug. 2004 that many juniors just "had fun" with the tests, making patterns when filling in the answer bubbles: "Christmas tree designs were popular. So were battleships and hearts."

11. **Testing is expensive and costs have increased since NCLB, placing a burden on state education budgets.** According to the Texas Education Agency, the state spent $9 million in 2003 to test students, while the cost to Texas taxpayers from 2009 through 2012 is projected to be around $88 million per year.

12. **The billion dollar testing industry is notorious for making costly and time-consuming scoring errors.** NCS Pearson, which has a $254 million contract to administer Florida's Comprehensive Assessment Test, delivered the 2010 results more than a month late and their accuracy was challenged by over half the state's superintendents. After errors and distribution problems in 2004–2005, Hawaii replaced test publisher Harcourt with American Institutes for Research, but the latter had to re-grade 98,000 tests after students received scores for submitting blank test booklets.

(Continued)

Table 3.1 Pro & Con Arguments: "Is the Use of Standardized Tests Improving Education in America?" (Continued)

PRO Standardized Tests	CON Standardized Tests
13. **Standardized tests provide a lot of useful information at low cost, and consume little class time.** According to a 2002 paper by Caroline M. Hoxby, PhD, the Scott and Donya Bommer Professor in Economics at Stanford University, standardized tests cost less than 0.1 percent of K–12 education spending, totaling $5.81 per student per year: "Even if payments were ten times as large, they would still not be equal to 1 percent of what American jurisdictions spend on education." Other cost estimates range from $15–$33 per student per year by the nonpartisan US Government Accountability Office (GAO), to as low as $2 per student per year by testing scholar and economist Richard P. Phelps. A fifty-item standardized test can be given in an hour and is graded instantaneously by computer.	13. **The multiple-choice format used on standardized tests is an inadequate assessment tool.** It encourages a simplistic way of thinking in which there are only right and wrong answers, which doesn't apply in real-world situations. The format is also biased toward male students, who studies have shown adapt more easily to the game-like point scoring of multiple-choice questions.
14. **Most teachers and administrators approve of standardized tests.** Minnesota teachers and administrators interviewed for a study in the Oct. 28, 2005, issue of the peer-reviewed Education Policy Analysis Archives (EPAA) approved of standardized tests "by an overwhelming two-to-one margin," saying they "improved student attitudes, engagement, and effort." An oft-cited Arizona State University study in EPAA's Mar. 28, 2002 edition, concluding that testing has little educational merit, has been discredited by educational researchers for poor methodology, and was criticized for wrongly blaming the tests themselves for stagnant test scores, rather than the shortcomings of teachers and schools.	14. **America is facing a "creativity crisis,"** as standardized testing and rote learning "dumb down" curricula and jeopardize the country's economic future. A 2010 College of William & Mary study found Americans' scores on the Torrance Test of Creative Thinking have been dropping since 1990, and researcher Kyung-Hee Kim lays part of the blame on the increase in standardized testing: "If we neglect creative students in school because of the structure and the testing movement . . . then they become underachievers."
15. **The multiple-choice format used on standardized tests produces accurate information necessary to assess and improve American schools.** According to the Center for Teaching Excellence at the University of Illinois at Urbana-Champaign, multiple-choice questions can provide "highly reliable test scores" and an "objective measurement of student achievement." Today's multiple-choice tests are more sophisticated than their predecessors. The Center for Public Education, a national public school advocacy group, says many "multiple-choice tests now require considerable thought, even notes and calculations, before choosing a bubble."	15. **Finland topped the international education (PISA) rankings from 2001 to 2008, yet has "no external standardized tests used to rank students or schools,"** according to Stanford University researchers Linda Darling-Hammond and Laura McCloskey. Success has been achieved using "assessments that encourage students to be active learners who can find, analyze, and use information to solve problems in novel situations."

16. **Stricter standards and increased testing are better preparing school students for college.** In Jan. 1998, Public Agenda found that 66 percent of college professors said "elementary and high schools expect students to learn too little." By Mar. 2002, after a surge in testing and the passing of NCLB, that figure dropped to 47 percent "in direct support of higher expectations, strengthened standards and better tests."

17. **Teacher-graded assessments are inadequate alternatives to standardized tests because they are subjectively scored and unreliable.** Most teachers are not trained in testing and measurement, and research has shown many teachers "consider noncognitive outcomes, including student class participation, perceived effort, progress over the period of the course, and comportment," which are irrelevant to subject-matter mastery.

18. **Cheating by teachers and administrators on standardized tests is rare, and not a reason to stop testing America's children.** The Mar. 2011 USA Today investigation of scoring anomalies in six states and Washington DC was inconclusive, and found compelling suggestions of impropriety in only one school. The US Department of Education's Office of Inspector General said on Jan. 7, 2013 that an investigation had found no evidence of widespread cheating on the DC Comprehensive Assessment System tests. It is likely that some cheating occurs, but some people cheat on their tax returns also, and the solution is not to abolish taxation.

16. **Excessive testing may teach children to be good at taking tests, but does not prepare them for productive adult lives.** China displaced Finland at the top of the 2009 PISA rankings because, as explained by Jiang Xueqin, Deputy Principal of Peking University High School, "Chinese schools are very good at preparing their students for standardized tests. For that reason, they fail to prepare them for higher education and the knowledge economy." China is trying to depart from the "drill and kill" test prep that Chinese educators admit has produced only "competent mediocrity."

17. **Using test scores to reward and punish teachers and schools encourages them to cheat the system for their own gain.** A 2011 USA Today investigation of six states and Washington DC found 1,610 suspicious anomalies in year-over-year test score gains. A confidential Jan. 2009 memo, prepared for the DC school system by an outside analyst and uncovered in Apr. 2013, revealed that 191 teachers in seventy DC public schools were "implicated in possible testing infractions," and nearly all the teachers at one DC elementary school "had students whose test papers showed high numbers of wrong-to-right erasures," according to USA Today. 178 Atlanta public school teachers from forty-four schools were found to be cheating on standardized tests according to a July 2011 state report. At one school, teachers attended "weekend pizza parties" to correct students' answers, according to ABC News.

18. **Standardized tests are an imprecise measure of teacher performance, yet they are used to reward and punish teachers.** According to a Sep. 2010 report by the Annenberg Institute for School Reform, over 17 percent of Houston teachers ranked in the top category on the Texas Essential Knowledge and Skills reading test were ranked among the two lowest categories on the equivalent Stanford Achievement Test. The results "were based on the same students, tested in the same subject, at approximately the same time of year, using two different tests."

(Continued)

Table 3.1 Pro & Con Arguments: "Is the Use of Standardized Tests Improving Education in America?" (Continued)

PRO Standardized Tests	CON Standardized Tests
19. **Each state's progress on NCLB tests can be meaningfully compared.** Even though tests are developed by states independently, state scores are compared with results on the National Assessment of Educational Progress (NAEP), ensuring each state's assessments are equally challenging and that gains in a state's test scores are valid.	19. **Each state develops its own NCLB standards and assessments, providing no basis for meaningful comparison.** A student sitting for the Connecticut Mastery Test (CMT) is asked a completely different set of questions from a child in California taking the Standardized Testing and Reporting (STAR) test, and while the former includes essay questions, the latter is entirely multiple-choice.
20. **State-mandated standardized tests help prevent "social promotion,"** the practice of allowing students to advance from grade to grade whether or not they have met the academic standards of their grade level. A Dec. 2004 paper by the Manhattan Institute for Policy Research found Florida's 2002 initiative to end social promotion, holding back students who failed year-end standardized tests, improved those students' scores by 9 percent in math and 4 percent in reading after one year.	20. **Open-ended questions on standardized tests are often graded by under-paid temporary workers with no educational training.** Scorers make $11–$13 per hour and need only a bachelor's degree, not necessarily related to education. As one former test scorer stated, "All it takes to become a test scorer is a bachelor's degree, a lack of a steady job, and a willingness to throw independent thinking out the window."
21. **Many objections voiced by the anti-testing movement are really objections to NCLB's use of test results, not to standardized tests themselves.** Prominent testing critic Diane Ravitch, Research Professor of Education at New York University, concedes standardized testing has value: "Testing . . . is not the problem . . . . information derived from tests can be extremely valuable, if the tests are valid and reliable." She cites the National Assessment of Educational Progress (NAEP) as a positive example, and says tests can "inform educational leaders and policy-makers about the progress of the education system as a whole."	21. **Schools feeling the pressure of NCLB's 100 percent proficiency requirement are "gaming the system" to raise test scores,** according to an Arizona State University report in the June 22, 2009, edition of the peer-reviewed *International Journal of Education Policy & Leadership*. Low-performing students are "encouraged to stay home" on test days or "counseled to quit or be suspended" before tests are administered. State education boards are "lowering the bar": manipulating exam content or scoring so that tests are easier for students to pass.
22. **Physicians, lawyers, real-estate brokers and pilots all take high-stakes standardized tests to ensure they have the necessary knowledge for their professions.** If standardized tests were an unreliable source of data, their use would not be so widespread.	22. **An obsession with testing robs children of their childhoods.** NCLB's mandate begins in third grade, but schools test younger students so they will get used to taking tests. Mar. 2009 research from the Alliance for Childhood showed "time for play in most public kindergartens has dwindled to the vanishing point, replaced by lengthy lessons and standardized testing." A three-year study completed in Oct. 2010 by the Gesell Institute of Human Development showed that increased emphasis on testing is making "children feel like failures now as early as PreK."

ProCon (2015) Is the use of standardized tests improving education in America? Retrieved from: http://standardizedtests.procon.org.

instructions from the test companies on what needs to be done to improve the scores.

The reality is that with the diversity in today's classrooms, standardized tests do not value nor take into consideration the variables of students. There are a wide range of differences in the people who take standardized tests. They have:

- Different cultural backgrounds
- Different levels of English proficiency
- Different learning and thinking styles
- Different family backgrounds
- Different past experiences

Standardized tests are designed to treat all students as if they were identical in every way. These assessments occur in a classroom where everything has either been taken down or covered. The tests are timed and the students cannot talk to each other even during bathroom breaks or lunchtime. The student cannot ask questions or clarify about what is being asked, and no references are allowed to be used. Since the main goal of today's education system is to prepare the student for the real world, most educators fail to see how this is achieving that. The only real life like this is prison!

It is also a fact that these tests provide parents and students with a false sense of security. Let's say a student scores the equivalent of 92 percent on the test. Parents, teachers, and the student would assume that they know the material. This, however, may not be the case. The student could have just memorized information but not have a working knowledge of how to apply it in real life. Much like a spelling test, the student would have known the word on Friday, but when asked to use it in a sentence the following week, the student would fail.

Standardized tests create "winners" and "losers." The data simply tells a teacher which are their "low students," "learning disabled kids," "gifted," or "reluctant learners." This label can cause the students to suffer from low self-esteem and lead them to believe in low expectations for themselves or always feeling like they have to do better in order to stay at the head of the class.

Let's look now at what standardized tests don't measure. They don't calculate a student's

- Creativity
- Critical thinking ability
- Resilience
- Motivation
- Persistence

- Curiosity
- Endurance
- Reliability
- Enthusiasm
- Empathy
- Self-awareness
- Self-discipline
- Honesty
- Leadership
- Civic mindedness
- Courage
- Compassion
- Resourcefulness
- Sense of beauty
- Sense of wonder
- Integrity

I can't speak for everyone, but aren't these the attributes we want our kids to have? It is common knowledge that a teacher can't really teach all of these from a textbook. They can, however, model them or talk with students about people who exemplify them. Unfortunately, this would require having time left over to do so after getting the kids ready to take the standardized test of achievement.

Chapter 4

So Why Do We Test?

What is education for? Is it for pouring facts and formulas into students' heads, or is it for creating learners? Today's students are coming to see school as the place to look smart and, above all, not look dumb—not a place to create and learn.

—Carol Dweck, PhD

THE BOTTOM LINE: PROFIT MARGIN

The existence of these tests is for administrative, political, and financial purposes, not for student achievement. The truth is that test companies make billions. Politicians use education and promises of better test scores as a platform for elections at the same time that school administrators receive funding, while also avoiding harsh penalties by boosting test scores. The net result: everyone benefits except the child. Standardized testing provides politicians a platform to display their concerns for the public school system. Through the use of political buzzwords such as accountability and the need for tougher standards, politicians reinforce demands for increased test scores.

Educational experts and politicians readily admit that the profit margin for NCLB tests is as low as 3 percent, but what they don't want you to know is that instructional materials such as textbooks, practice tests, workbooks, and other resources sold to the schools, which are prepared by the same companies that prepare the state tests, have up to a 21 percent profit margin.

According to Miner (2005), the largest companies that make up 96 percent of exam administration materials are as follows:

1. CTB McGraw-Hill, which in 2003 grossed over $3.8 billion in revenue ($566 million in net profits) and has contracts with twenty-three states (Miner, 2005). "With rapid expansion of its testing business to make up for lost revenues from its textbook segment, McGraw-Hill's state tests have been disrupted by 'glitches' in multiple states, affecting tens of thousands of students taking the high-stakes exams. The company has so far refused to sign the Student Privacy Pledge" (Persson, 2015).
2. Houghton Mifflin/Riverside Publishing contracts with twelve states and grosses more than $1 billion in sales yearly. According to Persson (2015):

   With revenues of $1.37 billion in fiscal year 2014, the company holds a 44% market share that includes some Common Core instructional resources and has its sights set on the pre-K testing and training market, crediting the federal government with creating "more opportunity in the early childhood market space from birth to eight" for revenue and profits. [Harcourt (*sic*) Mifflin told the Washington Post that "44 percent represents its 'addressable market share for U.S. instructional resources K-12,' which includes non-Common Core. The company also says it does not offer any high-stakes Common Core assessments."] (Persson, 2015)

3. Harcourt Brace Educational Measurement has contracts with eighteen states and in 2001 grossed over $5.6 billion (Miner, 2005).
4. Pearson, which is the largest corporation providing state testing and scoring systems, contracts with twenty-five states and brings in $9 billion annually. There is little competition for these companies and they have been dominating the market for years. Their education business accounts for more than 60 percent of earnings and sales and Pearson's total revenue is up 12 percent to $1.16 billion in 2012 (Figueroa, 2013).

Pearson also owns several publishers, including Adobe, Scott Foresman, Penguin, Longman, Wharton, Harcourt, Puffin, Prentice Hall, and Allyn & Bacon (among others). It also owns many tests like the National Assessment of Educational Progress (NAEP), the Stanford Achievement Test, the Millar Analogy Test, and the General Education Development (GED), as well as data systems such as Power School and SASI (Job, 2012).

Pearson not only writes the textbooks and tests that determine the curricula and instruction in public schools across the nation but also develops software that grades student essays, tracks student behavior, and provides criteria to diagnose not only ADD but also ways to treat it. Apart from these, it administers teacher licensing exams, coaches teachers in the classroom, counsels principals, and co-owns the for-profit company that administers the GED. And all this just covers the K–12 market (Simon, 2015).

Corporations exist to make profits. But shouldn't they also have to pay taxes? In Pearson's case, it was able to take advantage of the Hurricane Sandy tax deferral to significantly lower its 2012 U.S. tax bill (Singer, 2013). I want their tax preparer!

In 2012, a report by Brookings Institution found that $669 million in direct annual spending by forty-five states that participate is on assessment. This breaks down to approximately $27 a student (grades 3–9). However, when you add administrative costs involved in testing (like purchasing the materials in order for the students to "pass" the test), the total spending rises to $1100 per student . . . that's the part they don't want the public to know (Chingos, 2012). So, the companies that make the state-standardized, high-stakes tests are the ones that also publish the textbooks and resources that contain many of the answers to these tests . . . go figure!

Now let's add the test prep industry. Apart from tutoring, counseling, workbooks, and other educational programs designed to prepare kids for the test, parents spend $13.1 billion a year preparing their kids. "The private tutoring market accounts for another $78.2 billion a year. It is no wonder that school reform in the US attracts business people, not educators. When it comes to K–12 education in the US it is viewed as a $500 billion sector that is waiting desperately to be transformed by big break-throughs that extend the reach of great teaching" (Business Wire, 2010). The result: the United States has seen its largest "testing" arms race.

Texas, the second largest state, has led the testing craze, thanks to George W. Bush, a Texas native, and his hand in the passing of NCLB in 2002. What many are unaware of is that in 2000, Pearson Education, the company that produced tests for Texas, agreed to a $233 million contract to provide tests for schools in that state, and then renewed this agreement in 2005 for another $279 million. This continued with Gov. Rick Perry's appointment, and while Texas was slashing its education budget, he gave Pearson a $470 million contract "to come up with a new test that will hold Texas school children to a higher standard at the same time that budget cuts are forcing them into increasingly crowded classrooms" (Clawson, 2012).

"Texas alone paid Pearson $88,312,333 in the 2012–2013 school year which included $9 million for 'Program Management,' $3 million in 'quality Assurance,' $15 million in 'Test and Measurement' services and $9 million in 'Other Direct Costs'"(McDaniel, 2014). Pearson also owns the teacher performance assessment used for Texas Public School Districts and the GED testing rights.

Another example is that starting in 2010, Pearson Education has had a five-year contract with Texas worth $468 million for the STAAR test. "Texas has been the leader in standardized test adoption since 1979 and have doubled down on standardized tests every chance they could get to the point where in 2013 there were thirty-two tests and 15 percent of the final grade was based on standardized test results" (Akadjan, 2015).

This company also essentially runs the textbook market, as it has been given the right to have the last say on prices, which have been steadily rising. In an article published in *The Huffington Post* by Kingkade (2014), it was reported that college textbook prices have increased 812 percent over the past thirty years. That's more of an increase than college tuition over the same period of time. It has also been accused of publishing new editions of textbooks with little updated from the last edition and forcing students to buy new textbooks at inflated prices. As most know all too well, this results in the fact that when the time comes to sell back books to the bookstore at the end of the semester, only a fraction of the original price is made back (Kingkade, 2014). Therefore, it can be concluded that Pearson gets over half of its annual revenue from the U.S. colleges, and it is the students who bridge the gap.

While Pearson increases its profits through college students, it simultaneously pushes the U.S. education system into a corner. Through its support of the Common Core State Standards Initiative, which has developed a common standard for all state curriculums, job security is created by conveniently being heavily standardized test based. Guess where the funding and implementing of the standards came from? Pearson teamed up with the Gates Foundation! This has created a multimillion-dollar monopoly in the American education system. All this in order to turn over a profit, stripping both students and teachers of their freedom of expression and creativity in education (Spencer, 2013).

Spencer (2013) also reported that "between 2000 and 2012, Minnesota, Florida and Virginia among many other states, received millions of dollars in settlements from Pearson due to errors in test grading, and between 2005 and 2006, the company scored over 4,000 SAT college admission tests incorrectly." During its five-year contract with New York State, Pearson excluded thousands of eligible students for testing into gifted programs and of those that were tested, hundreds received incorrect scores.

Pearson is just one example of the for-profit companies that market their materials and design their standardized tests for states that are required by federal law to test their public school students in exchange for federal funding. This is a misaligned relationship that is only in the companies' interests and not those of the students, teachers, or schools. "The purpose is actually to make students and their educators to appear as if they are 'failing' so they can come in and offer their reform and solution resources and materials to states and districts for a healthy fee" (Matthews, 2015).

Much like the study of economics, when one firm controls both the supply and demand of its product, it creates a monopoly, which, unfortunately, has become the root of American marketing. These companies cash in irrespective of whether students pass or fail, but more so if students fail because then it would require schools to get more resources in order to help students pass. "The sad state of affairs created is that students, schools, districts and state education agencies have become profit centers for these corporations. In addition, these companies throw some of their profits to Washington, D.C. in order to hire lobbyists to ensure the Federal government doubles down on standardized testing" (Matthews, 2015).

If that wasn't enough, according to Piette (2014), "The Gates Foundation spent over $170 million to manipulate the U.S. Department of Education to impose the Common Core State Standardized testing (CCSS), knowing it would realize a return on this investment as school districts and parents buy the technology products that they have been brainwashed into believing were vital to improving education."

And yet the corruption continued as in 2011 and the Gates Foundation joined forces with Pearson in order to create new online reading and math courses for CCSS. This opened the door for Pearson to secure lucrative contracts in textbooks, testing, and software valued at tens of millions of dollars. "From 2009 to 2011 the Pearson Foundation contributed more than $540,000 to the Council of Chief State School Officers (CCSSO) to promote test development." This is in addition to the contracts Pearson already had with many states for testing under the NCLB law (Piette, 2014).

A Politico investigation discovered that "Pearson stands to make tens of millions in taxpayer dollars and provide cuts in student tuition based on deals arranged without competitive bids in states from Florida to Texas" (Simon, 2015). Also unveiled in this review is that within Pearson's contracts specific performance targets were embedded, which cleared Pearson of any penalties if the standards were not met. In addition, Pearson's higher education contracts give them extensive access to personal student data, with few constraints on how it is used (Simon, 2015).

Hundreds of pages of contracts, business plans, and email exchanges, as well as tax filings, lobbying reports, and marketing materials, were scoured during Politico's review. When the results were more closely reviewed, in the majority of the cases, Pearson was chosen primarily because the district was familiar with the company's name, not because the products were superior. One specific example found in the review was that of repetitive hiring in which the North Carolina Department of Public Instruction declined to even opt for competitive bids simply because Pearson had done work for the state in the past. Unfortunately, when this occurred, it caused the data system to be in such a disastrous state that the department had to pay Pearson millions extra to fix it (Simon, 2015).

Another example comes from the University of Florida where it was documented that administrators skipped collecting competitive bids on a huge project in order to build an online college from scratch. It seems the university officials were in a hurry to get the project started and since they were familiar with Pearson from another project, they felt Pearson was best suited for the job. "Even though the previous project was not overly successful, university officials dug up the old contract, and rewrote it giving Pearson the new job worth $186 million over the next decade" (Simon, 2015).

Also, two public colleges in Texas "not only gave Pearson a no-bid contract to build online classes, they agreed to pay the company to support 40,000 enrollments, no matter how many students actually signed up" (Simon, 2015).

Pearson has funds, aggressive lobbyists, a top-notch marketing team, and a highly skilled sales team. Fortunately, others are starting to notice that the country's obsession with high-stakes testing has allowed Pearson to get away with too much. In 2013, "the New York attorney general finally cracked down by prohibiting the company's charitable foundation from the practice of treating school officials from across the nation to trips abroad in order to attend conferences where the only education company represented was Pearson" (Simon, 2015). The bottom line: Pearson has taken over American education, but instead of students' best interests being high on its agenda, it is its profit margin that seems to matter the most.

Chapter 5

The Other Costs of Standardized Tests

Accountability makes no sense when it undermines the larger goals of education.

—Diane Ravitch

Curriculum across the nation has been narrowed due to the merging of state standards and assessments in order to measure and report student and school performance in response to the NCLB Act. Although it is claimed to focus on shining the light on student needs, it has resulted in a detour not only away from valuing the essential skills of persistence, but also towards avoiding critical thinking and collaboration. Standardized accountability has left the classroom teacher holding the bag for the performance of students and schools. As districts also pile on benchmark or practice standardized tests in order to track student performance levels and then factor in the increasing requirements for promotion and graduation, it is no wonder that teachers are leaving the public school system in massive numbers (Nelson, 2013).

It bothers many parents and educators that state legislators have decided that $500 million of taxpayers' money should go to the Pearson Corporation in the form of tests, and materials that support the tests, instead of going to schools for basic maintenance, roof repairs, or updated textbooks and technology. We are seeing an increasing number of schools becoming historic landmarks that are leaking and flooding and have technology in the form of wornout computers and overhead projectors, but by golly, we have testing booklets (Seaborn, 2015).

It also bothers most educators that every year, the children are being forced to take tests that are continually developmentally inappropriate for their age. One example is in the state of Texas where the content being mandated for use on the state test is not designed for the average mind of the child taking the test, making it difficult enough to process, let alone master, its content. The reality is that "elementary-aged kids are not abstract thinkers. This ability does not physiologically develop until roughly age twelve. Yet, this is the overwhelming theme of standardized exam prep materials. The problem is not that our kids are stupid and our teachers are ineffective. The problem is that these 'rigorous' concepts don't take hold in kids' minds if they are introduced too early" (Seaborn, 2015).

With the time teachers are taking to drill the test material, and take the practice benchmark tests, students are missing out on a tremendous amount of other things kids should be learning. Cursive writing is no longer taught or practiced, which can result in our future generations possibly not being able to even read the Constitution in its original form. This is a major piece of American history. Fewer and fewer districts are even able to hold on to an art and music program and even less than those are able to take educational field trips because of the severe budget cuts they are enduring. Any of the fun, creative, and cultural things have been stripped from the curriculum, leaving a dry skeleton of a template and lifeless students and teachers.

The computer age has seen a dramatic increase in videos and blogs from outstanding teachers who have had enough and are fleeing America's schools. These are the role models, the passionate and caring individuals, who have become tired of going the distance only to be slapped in the face with greater rigor and fewer resources instead of being celebrated for their dedicated service. Teachers with master skills in specific topics are being forced to abandon their expertise and valuable lessons because they do not fit the testing schedule that was designed by someone who could not teach a room full of students even if that person's life depended on it. "Educators can no longer be creative, imaginative, nor pay attention to individual students' needs and the student can't pursue things they may be interested in because they have to first memorize something for the test" (Chomsky, 2015).

Today's standardized tests have computer-based protocols that require the purchase of not only additional computers, but also increased bandwidth, for both of which the district must foot the bill from its operating budget. Some districts have reported spending upward of $18,000 to purchase new computers all to remain in compliance with the computerized testing requirements. This monetary figure does not include the electricity, data cables, network switch, and the furniture stations that also must be put into place and cost upwards to an additional $19,000. That is just for one lab at one school. "Regardless of whether the school or district bears the financial costs, high stakes testing harms the whole system by causing limited monetary resources to be spent, not on student learning and development, but merely on maintaining test requirements" (Strauss, 2012a).

Another cost is the fact that only certified personnel may assess students on the state standardized tests. This leaves K–2 teachers to be frequently called upon to administer tests, leaving their students to be served by substitute teachers. It is also the case that many special-area teachers such as Gifted, ESL, and Special Ed. must cancel their time with students in order to administer tests. School counselors are also called upon to administer tests and organize the testing materials. "This removes them from their priority tasks such as counseling students, monitoring graduation requirements, meeting with teachers and parents about student needs and leading the process of multi-tiered student services" (Strauss, 2012a). In addition, test coordinators are often mandated to receive yearly training after school and then set up a schedule to train the test administrators and proctors on the campus. Many times, in order to attend training, they must revise work schedules and often have to arrange childcare for their own school-aged children (Strauss, 2012a).

In most cases, the teachers who are not testing are required to move from their classrooms in order to accommodate test sites. Test coordinators also require these teachers to remove or cover instructional materials (that can be extensive) from students' sight (word walls, or other graphic organizers, sometimes, even the clocks had to be covered!) as required by the testing mandates. With the rigorous testing schedule and the large numbers of students who must be tested, schools pay the ultimate price of disruptions in the learning environment in order to provide optimum testing settings. The secure testing environment takes precedence over student learning, leaving students without their teachers of record to conduct lessons, rendering them without visitors such as parents to join them for lunch, and often being removed to sections of the building such as labs or the library that are not conducive to learning.

Another impact testing has on student learning is the fact that, in a single year, as many as sixty-two tests may be administered by a district to its students. If you do the math, this means that students will spend a minimum of nine weeks in kindergarten through second grade and up to twenty-one weeks in the upper grades (3–12) testing. Anyone with so many tests for core subjects would lose their momentum. Even if you are a parent of a student in a non-tested grade level, your child is not safe from the effects of testing. "When media centers, reading labs, science rooms and computer labs are not housing non testing students, they remain closed to the entire school, negatively impacting the academic programs for K-12 students" (Strauss, 2012a).

This, combined with the hours educators spend combing over the testing data, accounts for even more lost learning time for students. This data is then used to make promotion and graduation decisions which can have psychological and social issues for students who are much older than their grade-level peers, resulting in potential safety issues for younger students. For example, take a sixteen-year-old who, because of retention based on standardized test results, is attending a middle school with eleven-year-old sixth graders. According to Strauss (2012), "Research demonstrates that retained students remain the lowest performers in the grade level. Retention does not improve student achievement."

Another testing reality is the fact that results from all this testing come back oftentimes during the summer months. This often causes promotion decisions for some students being postponed until after school is out, causing teachers to not be able to make final promotion decisions about every student in a timely manner. Since teachers are off contract time during the summer, principals are left to contact parents to advise them that even though their final report card showed promotion, the student may still be retained. For those who are contracted to work during the summer months, much of their time is spent analyzing data and organizing the test results into the student cumulative folders instead of finalizing the year's paperwork and preparing for the upcoming academic year.

Most educators will admit that the content of standardized tests is not aligned with typical classroom instruction and behavior because it has to be generalized. This results in the fact that teachers have to modify their teaching practices and the focus of their classroom instruction in order to prepare students adequately for the tests. They are forced to narrow the curriculum and focus on the core subjects that are tested and minimize other learning activities such as art and physical education. Teachers are also finding themselves devoting more time to memorization rather than critical thinking and learning, which as we all know, lowers the quality of instruction.

In a report by the American Federation of Teachers (AFT, 2013), two unnamed medium-sized school districts, one in the Midwest and one in the East, were researched in terms of their standardized testing calendars. It was discovered that "test prep and testing absorbed nineteen full school days in one district and a month and a half in the other in heavily tested grades" (AFT, 2013). In addition, the Midwestern district spent $600 or more for standardized testing per pupil in grades 3–8; about $200 per student for grades K–2; from $400 to $600 per student for grades 9–11. The Eastern district spent more than $1,100 annually on testing per student in grades 6–11; around $400 per student in grades 1–2; between $700 and $800 per student for grades 3–5 (AFT, 2013).

According to Strauss (2013), the AFT report also says:

- In the high testing grades (3–11), it is possible that a student can spend from sixty to 110 hours per year in test preparation.

- Including the cost of lost instructional time, the per pupil cost of annual testing can range from $700 to more than $1,000 for grades that have multiple tests.

This report also concluded that if testing were abandoned, "one school district in this study could add from twenty to forty minutes of instruction to each school day for most grades. The other school district would be able to add almost an entire class period to the school day for grades 6–11" (Strauss, 2013). Imagine, documented proof of how students are being robbed of valuable instructional and learning time and yet policymakers and educational leaders implement more testing in our schools.

Chapter 6

How Is the Increase in Child Poverty Affecting Standardized Testing?

Those born into less privileged social and economic circumstances are punished at least twice: first, when they start life already behind their more privileged peers; and second, when the testing game's sorting, labeling, and screening of children begins.

—Peter Sacks

Much of the mainstream media focuses on the usual school reform debate and seldom addresses the role of poverty in student achievement. Those reformers who do acknowledge student poverty claim it is no excuse for teachers in accomplishing bad standardized test scores. Few reformers defend the fact that outside influences matter more and a single teacher can do little to overcome them in order to increase student scores.

Today's public schools have seen an explosion in the enrollment of students living in poverty. Teachers are witness to an increase in students sleeping in class, having severe asthma attacks, and coming to school with their basic needs not being met. These have a tremendous effect on all aspects of a child's school experience. The rise in the number of children living in poverty comes at a time when there is tremendous pressure to increase scores on standardized tests and creates great challenges for public schools.

Hunger has many effects on children, which can include headaches, stomachaches, colds, ear infections, and fatigue. These effects can lead to it taking longer for them to recover. Poverty often leads to a lack of healthy food in the home, which can affect a child's ability to concentrate and thus lead to him or her performing poorly in school. Such children also have a higher tendency to suffer from behavioral, emotional, and academic problems and can often become more aggressive and anxious (Texas Classroom Teachers Association [TCTA], 2014).

The effects of poverty, however, go beyond hunger. The ability for a student from a low-income home to achieve academically is drastically affected. For various reasons, including lack of parental education and fewer opportunities, fewer words are heard in the home, which leads to limited vocabulary when children enter school. Lower income also results in fewer books and other resources in the home as well as the lack of being able to provide those real-world experiences that help build background knowledge that households with more income can provide (TCTA, 2014).

When you subject an economically disadvantaged student to the rigors of standardized testing, it creates a very challenging situation for today's teacher. According to TCTA (2014), "During the 2012–2013 school year, 69 percent of economically disadvantaged students in the state of Texas passed all subjects in all grades compared to the state average of 77 percent. The economically disadvantaged student subgroup has a lower passing rate than the state average on every test."

The lack of opportunity to build background knowledge plays a big role in the success on standardized testing. Test language is one factor that plays a part in it, as the formal registry used on the tests presents a huge struggle for economically disadvantaged children as well as those for whom English is not their first language. Teachers also face challenges in helping students who do not bring the necessary skills to their classroom. Not only are these children financially deprived, but most also lack social skills and/or knowledge of the "hidden rules" of social groups. These are only some of the demands that are forcing teachers to move into specialized jobs such as counselors, interventionists, and administration simply because the challenges have become so overwhelming in the classroom (TCTA, 2014).

Now let's add the move to tie students' test scores to teacher evaluations and imagine the negative effect on the teaching profession. "Many teachers and other stakeholders in public education say student performance on standardized tests is an invalid measure of a teacher's effectiveness in which research states that teaching accounts for less than 15 percent of student achievement outcomes while socioeconomic factors account for 60 percent" (TCTA, 2014).

The truth is that family income affects student background knowledge, and it is this prior knowledge that test scores truly reflect, not students' ability to learn and achieve. Teachers may have achieved amazing progress with some of their students (I have witnessed two or more years' growth of students in the 180-day school calendar), but because the students started so far behind, it is not going to get them to proficient levels on the test. So, why shouldn't the teacher be rewarded for the progress made instead of being punished for low test scores? Maybe if teachers were valued more for their hard work, they would stay in the profession longer and not shy away from where they are needed most.

Policy and decision makers need to quit relying so much on schools to mitigate the factors of poverty and spend their time, money, and efforts finding ways to improve life for the tremendous number of people living below the poverty line. By offering jobs that provide health insurance, sick days, and livable wages for parents, schools would see fewer students being sent to school sick because their parents cannot afford to take the day off or to pay for proper child care.

The fact is that there is not one single factor that can be blamed for the growing achievement gap. Low income is only one category in the variables that affect students' ability to be successful on tests. There are, however, a complex set of socioeconomic factors that definitely contribute to educational access and until these factors get the attention they need to be resolved, teachers and schools will be labeled with derogatory names and blamed for the outcome of our children.

Corporate education reformers thrive on the platform that poverty is not an excuse for failure because it goes against the myth of mediocrity and continues to reinforce the privatization movement in order to improve schools. This stance, however, avoids addressing the inequities that exist in our society that are reinforced by school structure.

This "no-excuses" hot air actually hurts poor children living in poverty. Standardized tests arguably have cultural and racial biases, and with the increase in ELLs and special needs students, failing schools are being forced to close, leaving students with no other choice but to move out of their home communities. All these variables overlap in low-performing schools and largely dictate educational access for these students. These schools are often not funded equitably and result in being more likely to have large class sizes; too many teachers without subject area certification; and inadequate books, libraries, laboratories, computers, and other facilities. In addition, many of the low-poverty students also suffer problems with housing, nutrition, or health care. The question is, "Are high-stakes tests punishing them for things they cannot control?"

It shouldn't be surprising that "the challenging working conditions have resulted in teacher shortages leaving high poverty schools with a higher rate of teachers that are on an emergency license, alternatively certified, teaching out of their subject area, brand new, or yes, 'ineffective'" (Strauss, 2012b).

High-poverty schools also have a higher level of bureaucracy, which results in a decrease of human capital. This also contributes to the excessive movement of teachers, which not only costs schools tons of money but also has a detrimental effect on students who can't afford any more contributions to the achievement gap (Strauss, 2012b).

Many factors are influenced when a school is located in a low-income area. Low-income student populations tend to influence higher mobility rates and absentee rates, and many social issues—like hunger/malnutrition, abuse, homelessness, incarcerated parents, deported parents, crowded homes with no privacy, drugs, crime, and so on—can affect students' mental, physical and emotional well-being in the classroom. Since these characteristics vary from community to community, it is impossible to create a general list (Strauss, 2012b).

For politicians and policy makers to place the blame on so-called "ineffective" teachers and "failing schools" is an easy way out. Their energies should be redirected and replaced with the adoption of a complex analysis of the socio-cultural-economic factors that influence a child's school experience (Strauss, 2012b). By not doing that, "deeply ingrained inequalities in our society and the structural design of schools (which help perpetuate that inequality) remain able to go unchecked while the focus becomes 'accountability,' firing teachers, and closing schools" (Strauss, 2012b). Another tragedy is that by not redirecting the focus of education, what remains is the stigma of a one-size-fits-all approach.

This reminds me of the Beatles song lyrics, "Imagine there's no heaven." Imagine a system of education that doesn't close schools and fire teachers, but actually provides resources and services that actually meet the needs of the students, and offers teachers relevant mentoring and professional development. These are the types of initiatives that need to be put into place in order to make real reforms happen to address poverty in our schools. Anything else is a mere Band-Aid.

SCORES DROP WITH TEST CHANGES

According to Northington (2008), during the 2005–2006 school term, the Louisiana Education Department changed from the Iowa Test of Basic Skills exam to the Integrated Louisiana Educational Assessment Program (iLEAP) exam for the third, fifth, sixth, seventh, and ninth grades. The format of the iLEAP test consists of a combination of the LEAP and Iowa tests. The Iowa test was composed of mostly multiple-choice questions, while the iLEAP test, although has multiple-choice questions, also consists of a writing portion and parts where students solve math problems in the test booklet (Northington, 2008).

History has proven that anytime there is a change in a testing format there is an automatic drop in scores. In reality, it usually takes about three to five years to get the kids used to the new test and then the scores go back up. This is primarily due to the fact that when the test changes, the scoring method also changes. In this particular case, instead of the iLEAP combined score making up a small percentage of the school's performance score, it now made up about a third of the total performance rating. Although poverty is a factor in the nationwide decrease of school scores, it is not the only factor.

POVERTY LIMITS OPPORTUNITY

Poverty has many definitions. For the purpose of this book, it is referred to as persons with income less than that deemed sufficient to purchase basic needs such as food, shelter, clothing, and other essentials. The reality is that it is complex, and does not mean the same thing for all people. The 2014 U.S. poverty guidelines reveal that the cutoff for poverty in a two-person household is $15,730 per year (Miller, 2015). For public schools, poverty is defined by students' enrollment in the federally funded free and/or reduced-price meal program. To qualify, a family of four must have a household income of less than $26,845 to recieve free meals or $38,203 to receive reduced-price meals.

Let's face it. In every school, there are students whose parents are able to provide opportunities for their children. This exposure helps build student background knowledge and can help accelerate learning. For those who do not have these experiences, it makes it much harder to relate to things and perform well on tests. Most schools with high poverty levels have implemented the administration of pretests at the beginning of the school year in order to be proactive in identifying weaknesses of students. Once these have been identified, teachers can then develop lessons that target specific skills in core subjects and access special software to help bring students up to grade-level proficiency. Though some schools have lost ground when enrolling more poor students, educators say poverty does not affect students' ability to learn but may limit their opportunities (Northington, 2008).

Let me be perfectly clear. This is not to say that children of poverty are not intelligent; they just have many miles to go because of lack of opportunities.

HIGH-POVERTY SCHOOLS GET HELP

It is often the case that high-poverty, low-performing schools receive additional money from the federal government on the basis of their free/reduced-price meal program enrollment. The most recognized form of federal assistance to schools is known as Title 1 Funding. This money allows schools to purchase additional resources for children in the form of additional teachers, after-school programs, and basic school supplies. According to Biddle and Berliner (2002), "The majority of schools that received this funding have earned significant school performance score improvement since 2002."

Unfortunately, regardless of the improved scores, these schools still carry a stigma of being ineffective and face the charge that their classrooms are filled with chaos. Nothing could be farther from the truth. These schools are usually free from any chaos and are structured, and where learning is more focused.

Chapter 7

How Is the Increase in Cultural Diversity Affecting Standardized Testing?

A school's culture has more influence on life and learning in the schoolhouse than the president of the country, the state department of education, the superintendent, the school board, or even the principal, teachers, and parents can ever have.

—Roland Barthes

Just because some students score higher than others on a test does not make it biased. A biased test is when the scores of one group are significantly different and have a higher future performance prediction than another group. Most test biases are considered cultural biases. "Cultural bias is the extent to which a test offends or penalizes some students based on their ethnicity, gender or socioeconomic status" (Hurst, 2015).

TYPES OF BIAS

Basically, the fact that differential performance between and among groups exists is where bias concerns originate. The question of why one group performs differently than another on a consistent basis leaves concerns as to the individual characteristics of examinees, the testing environment, and/or characteristics of the test or test items needing to be answered.

Hurst (2015) goes on to explain the different types of test biases that affect the accuracy and usability of the test results.

Bias in Construct Validity. Bias in construct validity is present when a test is shown to measure different hypothetical constructs or traits for one group versus another; this type of bias also exists when the test measures the same trait for groups but with differing degrees of accuracy. The primary question is: Does the item or test measure what it is intended to measure? One example of this has to do with a child's first language. Testing a second language learner whose first language is not English can be problematic if the child is not proficient. This can cause an achievement test to become a language test, in which the child may actually know the correct answer to the question, but because of the language barrier, cannot understand what is being asked.

Bias in Content Validity. This bias is due to a student's lack of exposure or experience and therefore is at a disadvantage of how to correctly answer a question. For example, if a student is asked the question, "How are basketball and football alike?" a student or group who has never played, watched, or had discussions about basketball is at a disadvantage. Reynolds (1998) lists three examples of content bias:

- The items ask for information that minority persons have not had the same experience or opportunity to learn as others.
- The scoring of the item is inappropriate. In other words, a member of a minority group may be penalized for giving an answer that does not match the answer key, but would be correct in his or her culture.
- The wording or registry used in the questions are unfamiliar, whereas the student may know the correct answer but is not able to understand what is being asked or has no experience with the test format.

Bias in Item Selection. Item selection is considered biased when the items and tasks selected are based on the learning experiences and language of the dominant group. Although this form of bias resembles content validity, item selection involves appropriateness of the actual items on the test. It does not require that the overall test be statistically biased, but only a few specific items can be so. One example would be in the concern of how one item gets included on a test but another does not.

Bias in Predictive or Criterion-Related Validity. Refers to the accuracy of a test in the prediction of how well a certain student group will perform. The focal question here is: "Does the test score accurately predict how the student or group will perform on a task in the future?" Many times, a high IQ score is affiliated with a high grade point average and indicates success in both college and a career path. A test is considered "unbiased if the results for all relevant subpopulations cluster equally well around a single regression line . . . an unbiased test predicts performance equally for all groups, even though their means may be different" (Gregory, 2004, p. 244).

The bottom line is that there is a danger involved when we use standardized testing based on white middle-class children as the measurement by which to judge other children. Until testing separates culture from development, poor and minority children will continue to be overrepresented in early intervention, special education, and at-risk programs. Educators also need more training in what characteristics are attributed to developmental delays versus cultural differences. It is unfortunate that because of the pressures of standardized testing results, teachers are simply left with the perception that if the child were normal, they would have learned to perform the specific task.

Standardized testing has been misused for decades. Students have been misplaced in special programs due to the results on a screening test. The problem is that most educators have no idea of the linguistic environment in which their students live and provide intervention that emphasizes the slowing down and oversimplifying of language for all students as if they were all equally developmentally disabled. Oftentimes, this results in wrong treatment, especially for the culturally different child, who is capable of learning in a normalized language environment.

Let's face it. We are all victims of our own past experiences, and teachers are no exception. Like all of us, they make generalizations about people based on their personal experiences and reality. According to Ball (1989), "Teachers have difficulty incorporating new visions of reality that conflict with their own personal beliefs and experiences. It is human nature that we cling to our own theories forcing contrary evidence to fit our own beliefs. It follows then that when behavior does not fit preconceived notions, we manipulate it to conform to our sense-making hypotheses."

As you can well imagine, it is rare that adults and children share common experiences or hold common beliefs about their meaning. "This leaves them apt to misunderstand culturally encoded interchanges" (Bowman, 1994). Within this theory lies the reasoning as to why teachers fail to appreciate real similarities and differences between their perceptions of their world and those of the students who come from different backgrounds. In a sense, teachers become victims of their own naïve conceptions of culture.

Many children are faced with the challenge of distinguishing between home and school in terms of qualities of interpersonal relationships, behavior standards, and objectives of education. Differences in how these are expressed can be confusing for anyone, but especially for a child. For example, a child brought up in a culture that values physical aggression and what is known as "macho" behavior may find it difficult to suppress this behavior in the school setting. This behavior can also cause a child that has been raised in a more conservative socialization to feel threatened when it experiences this aggression. Neither child's beliefs are wrong; they simply reflect the normal development process of identification with the values and behaviors of family and friends. Let me be clear, I am not defending whether high or low levels of aggression are desirable; I am only stating that it may be viewed as normal in some cultural communities. When schools value low aggression, they must also be aware that this can set the stage for cultural conflict for those who believe physical aggression can reflect competence and effectiveness.

In addition, racism and classism also play a factor in causing conflict between school and poor minority children and their families. One such example is how the representation of Anglocentric and middle-class viewpoints devalues students and families from other cultures such as Spanish-speaking children (Bowman, 1994). In the case of ELLs, it is more of a situation in which the students, their families, and communities are undervalued instead of being supported in order to increase self-esteem and confidence. An even more serious result is that when teachers devalue the culture of poor and minority children, they are encouraging an ominous cultural choice: either identify with family and friends and disavow the school, or embrace school culture and face emotional/social isolation. "The result is that many young children opt for family and friends and become unwilling participants in school culture" (Bowman, 1994).

According to Ogbu (1992), these students are more likely to be less motivated to learn skills associated with the white middle class, since their efforts will not pay off with the same opportunities that others derive. What they end up doing is developing oppositional practices that will separate them further from the mainstream which, in turn, affects their school achievement and most likely results in a loss of peer affiliation and support (Ogbu, 1992).

When a student lives in an environment where adults are authoritarian, personal, and expressive and then encounter teachers who are indirect, impersonal, and do not react to emotional displays, it results in students spending the majority of their time testing the teacher's limits instead of learning the content being taught. According to FairTest (2008), the past few decades have shown that African-American, Latino, and Native American students experience many problems with high-stakes testing from early childhood through to college entrance. For these students, tests provide no social or educational benefit. Unfortunately, not receiving a diploma can lead to a future containing higher rates of unemployment and an increased chance of imprisonment.

Many times students who score low on tests are held back in grade. This retention often undermines self-esteem and increases the likelihood of the student dropping out of school. Low SAT and ACT scores are causing talented youth to be denied entrance into college and access to scholarships, which increases the racial gap in college enrollment and completion (FairTest, 2008).

The effects of high-stakes testing for many students of color who are ELLs are even more damaging. One example is in the tests that are given in

Spanish where the translation is often inaccurate and results in more confusion for the student. This often leads to misplacement in programs as these ELLs are placed in classrooms with students who have learning disabilities or retention, which creates a defeating environment and lessens the likelihood of them passing graduation tests. This is the direct result of the negative reputation that immigrant students face in our schools about their academic achievement.

It seems in today's society, the more a person's culture differs from the dominant culture in which he or she lives, the greater that person's learning will be adversely affected. The bottom line is that if a child is to benefit from instruction, the language of that instruction must be drawn from the child's existing cultural and linguistic foundations. As educators, we know that diversifying instruction in order to celebrate various cultures as assets in the classroom is key to increased understanding and learning. As long as standardized testing remains centered around the Anglo middle-class population, the results of efforts of educators will remain the same as beating their heads against a brick wall.

Chapter 8

What Do Standardized Tests Actually Reflect?

We are raising today's children in sterile, risk-averse and highly structured environments. In so doing, we are failing to cultivate artists, pioneers and entrepreneurs, and instead cultivating a generation of children who can follow the rules in organized sports games, sit for hours in front of screens and mark bubbles on standardized tests.

—Darell Hammond

"Teachers teach, learners learn, and standardized tests monitor how well the process is going" (Strauss, 2014) or at least that is what policy makers and politicians would have us believe. "Standardized tests take the amount of information that was taught and subtract the amount not learned or learned and forgotten in order to obtain a quantity or score. The score provides a number for sorting and labeling not only the kids, but teachers, schools, school systems, states and nations" (Futterman, 2015).

In 2011, Secretary of Education Arne Duncan announced it was possible that 82 percent of the U.S. schools could be failing by the end of 2012. This created the lingering questions: What are we testing and how are we doing it? Educational policy and decision makers would like you to believe that standardized testing is a direct result of scientific nature, but in reality, they are nothing alike.

Whereas an item can be measured and weighed, standardized tests are objective only in the sense that they are scored by a machine. They are subjective in the fact that they are created by human beings. People write the questions, which opens the door to varying interpretations, biases, or even irrelevance, depending on who is choosing the items to include.

Those who support standardized tests argue that it is unrealistic to think schools can eliminate the need for such tests. It is sad that many do not realize that these tests are based on unrealistic exercises that do not apply to the real world. The real question is: What are these tests doing to prepare students for life outside the classroom? I am not defending standardized tests here, at least not in the way they are utilized in the majority of states. I do agree, however, that schools do need an objective measure of student achievement.

Another debate is in the fact as to whether the tests actually indicate achievement or do they tend to be more accurate indicators of whether a child lives above or below the poverty line? Some research has indicated that "the amount of poverty found in a community, and other factors having absolutely nothing to do with the daily events in the classroom, account for the majority of differences in test scores from one area to another" (Pollard, 2002).

Looking at the three approaches to teaching—telling, showing, and involving—it concludes that the one that is most successful is involving the learner. What really needs to be evaluated are the outcomes based on personal experiences, and not machine-scored test items. When educators move beyond reading about plants and provide opportunities for students to go outside in order to identify, examine, and classify what is growing around the playground, learning takes place and becomes relevant. Worksheets are a thing of the past in the involved classroom where students study force in motion by creating various inclines and racing marbles in order to find out how height affects its speed.

The reality is that teachers who are practicing the involved method of learning are usually the older, well-seasoned educators. Unfortunately, high-stakes testing is even forcing these experienced teachers to simply guess what is probably going to be on the test and proceed to hammering it into kids relentlessly. Experiences that create understanding? Our education system has seen standardized test scores dictate what happens to students, teachers, administrators, and the school. Making sure students understand and learn takes a back seat to filling in the right bubble on an answer sheet.

But what does this standardized test reveal about the child? "In the case of colleges and schools, these tests measure intelligence and how prepared they are to do college level work" (Goldshteyn, 2014). Merriam-Webster defines *intelligence* as "the ability to learn or understand things or to deal with new or difficult situations" ("Intelligence", n.d.). Nowhere in this definition do we see that this ability is limited to reading, science, and math but is left wide open and can include playing an instrument or sport, debating a topic of which they are passionate, or developing knowledge about their world. Policy makers and other educational decision makers need to realize how narrowed we are making the minds of future students, as none of these extracurricular things are measured on a standardized test.

Teachers know that the bottom line is simply that the only thing these tests measure is a student's ability to concentrate when they're nervous, memorize information, and whether they are a good test taker. This leaves successful scorers to be those that have a great memory and know key strategies on how to approach questions while others with test anxiety or poor memories, but still very intelligent, to fail. Thus, standardized tests benefit only one type of individual, while all others are at a disadvantage (Goldshteyn, 2014).

So in short, the reality of standardized tests is that they don't completely measure intelligence, but rather your memorization skills and your abilities to pick the right answer from a choice of four possibilities. Another consequence is when a student can simply not afford a tutor for their SATs or enroll in a prep course for review. It goes without saying that those who can afford it, do better on the test. This leaves one to wonder, however, about all the students who are in public schools who are left to face the enormous numbers of tests they must endure.

According to Strauss (2012), several schools have opted not to look at test scores as criteria for acceptance into college. Since 2010, eighty colleges have broken ground by not requiring SAT and ACT tests to be taken in order for entrance. They are claiming that a better indicator of students' abilities is their high-school grades. A few of the colleges included in this eighty are New York University, University of Texas, and the Worcester Polytechnic Institute.

Thus, colleges agree a good test helps assess a student's progress, but by no means is it the only tool. A standardized test can show several things, including:

- Students' knowledge in comparison with grade level or common core standards
- Tracking the year-to-year development of a student
- The academic strengths and weaknesses of students
- A comparison to other students within a campus or across campuses
- How effective a curriculum or specific teaching method was

According to Wai (2014), "The tests do provide information about where people stand on critical skills and provides students with guidance in vocation and admissions decisions." These skills affect many different facets of life to a much greater degree than most believe. The issue is that the extra effort it takes to perform well on these tests means that students have sacrificed time to focus on their actual schoolwork, especially in high school.

HOW DO SCHOOLS USE STANDARDIZED TESTS?

Each type of standardized test has a different purpose. One format is the standardized achievement test which typically is used to measure how much students have already learned about a school subject. Teachers can use this data in order to develop programs that fit students' achievement level across content or subject matter.

Another format is the standardized aptitude test. This measures students' abilities to learn in school in order to predict how well they are likely to perform in future school work. According to Project Appleseed (2014), "Instead of measuring knowledge of subjects taught in school, these tests measure a broad range of abilities or skills that are considered important to success in school." Some of the skills they measure include a student's verbal ability, mechanical ability, creativity, clerical ability, or abstract reasoning. This information is then used by teachers' plan instruction that is aligned to the students' levels. Project Appleseed (2014) also states that some of the other uses for these tests by schools, teachers, and districts include:

- School program evaluation
- Tracking student progress
- Individual or groups of students' strengths and weaknesses
- Special program selection
- Differentiating instruction or creating intervention groups
- Deciding student promotion or graduation

According to Weiss (2012), standardized exams aren't very specific at identifying the effects of classroom instruction. He states that "less than 30 percent of the differences in student scores can be related to content knowledge, teaching skill, and differences in curriculum design." But even with this knowledge, the tests are the main criteria used by a majority of states in the rating of the effectiveness of teachers, schools, and school districts.

Most testing companies do not want the public to know or understand that standardized tests are scored on a "normed" scale which is purposely created so that half the students will score below the fifth percentile and the other half will score above. This creates a nationally normed group sampling of students that reflects the demographics of the U.S. students in a specific age group. The problem with this system is that some states with very diverse populations cannot produce an exact match to the nationally normed group. This totally discredits any comparison that a standardized test can develop between the two different student population samples and can result in a very compelling debate concerning the kinds of educational programs that may be necessary to meet the needs of these varying groups of students. This makes it next to impossible for educators to successfully refine instruction and identify program changes.

Because standardized testing ignores higher-level thinking skills, it creates an environment in which students become superficial thinkers who seek a quick, easy, and obvious answer.... To reinforce this, one only needs to refer to Koretz (2008), who states that there are two reasons tests do not provide a direct and complete measure of educational achievement. First, tests can measure only a portion of the goals of education, which are necessarily broader and more inclusive than the test could possibly be. Most parents would agree this is far from the achievements they expect from their child. Education officials and policy makers mean well when they emphasize achievement, but their definition of achievement clearly means test scores, and only test scores. They do not account for a student's motivation, reliability, enthusiasm, critical thinking, creativity, or resilience, which are really the qualities that young adults need to develop in order to be successful in this world. It is also unfortunate that they rarely take into account the fact that in order to have a good understanding of students' development there are other forms of information that educators and parents need to know, such as how children are growing physically and emotionally as well as intellectually. Information from test scores is very limited and educators need to be careful before drawing conclusions about what a score on an assessment means.

The second reason Koretz (2008) cites for the incompleteness of test scores as a measure of achievement is: "Even in assessing the goals that can be measured well, tests are generally very small samples of behavior that we use to make estimates of students' mastery of very large domains of knowledge and skill." This concludes that not only are they not doing a good job of measuring achievement in terms of creativity and persistence, it includes only a small part of specific domains that are on the assessment, which can be dangerous if this information is the only data used to draw inferences about our children.

Chapter 9

Are There Benefits to Standardized Testing?

> *Making students accountable for test scores works well on a bumper sticker and it allows many politicians to look good by saying that they will not tolerate failure. But it represents a hollow promise. Far from improving education, high stakes testing marks a major retreat from fairness, from accuracy, from quality and from equity.*
>
> —Senator Paul Wellstone

Most would agree that any assessment that provides dependable information about important outcomes is useful. One example is the weekly spelling test that covers a specific grammatical rule like plurals of words that end in y. The results of these tests can provide information to teachers, parents, and students as to whether the concept was learned.

The disagreement comes in the usefulness of statewide testing. Those people deciding the content of these tests claim to have an interest in improving education. These committees consist of teachers, curriculum experts, parents, and (occasionally) representatives from business and industry who are faced with the challenge of determining what the most important things a specific grade-level student should know or be able to do in mathematics, reading, and science. "Once decided, the answers to these questions are then translated into a framework for the statewide test, which is really just a list of those outcomes judged to be most important" (Cizek, 2000).

My confusion is, like many of us, if the group truly represented the community and if high expectations are reflected in their outcome decisions, then most would agree that the results of the test could genuinely give a more complete picture as to whether students have genuinely accomplished important goals, how individual and groups of students compare to each other, and how well a campus or district performs overall. Unfortunately, this is not the case.

According to Roediger et al. (2011) the following are five benefits of standardized testing:

Benefit 1: Retrieval aids later retention. There is clear evidence from psychological experiments that practicing retrieval of something after learning it, for instance by taking a quiz or test, makes you more likely to retain it for the long term.

Benefit 2: Gaps in knowledge can be identified by testing. A test lets all involved be aware of what a student knows and what they do not know. One such example is when students take a pretest, find out which questions they got wrong, and then restudy those items in order to take a final test (Son and Kornell, 2008). "Testing one's memory allows one to evaluate whether the information is really learned and accessible" (Roediger et al., 2011).

Benefit 3: How to study can be enhanced when a study receives test results. After students have restudies for a test previously taken, they gain experience of the question format and topics and therefore learn more from the presentation than if they would not have taken the pretest. "Feedback is provided after the test and this condition greatly out spaces the restudy-only condition even when timing parameters are equated" (McDermott and Arnold, 2010).

Benefit 4: Students learn how to organize their knowledge through testing experiences. As students restudy for a test, they learn to organize the important information and details for easier recall. Open-ended and essay questions become easier to answer because students have organized the information into practical conceptual facts. In other words, testing can increase both category clustering and subjective organization of materials compared to restudying.

Benefit 5: The transferring of knowledge to connect with new context can be improved through testing. "Retrieval practice induces readily accessible information that can be flexibly used to solve new problems. Practicing retrieval has been shown time and time again to produce enhanced memory later for tested material" (Butler, 2010).

Cascio (2015) is in agreement that there are several benefits of the standardized testing format. These benefits are discussed in the following sections.

UNIFORM ASSESSMENT

The same standardized test is given to every student, which allows educators to use them as trustworthy standards of measurement in the evaluation of student performance. The data from these tests identifies a student's strengths and weaknesses as well as how they compare to their classmates, making it easier for the struggling student to be identified. These tests show how students progress from year to year as well as show the state which schools are the most successful in meeting the state standards for each grade level. The data also shows which schools are experiencing the most difficulty in meeting those standards.

PRACTICAL APPLICATION

The convenience of standardized tests is an advantage for both schools and students. The tests take only a few hours to administer in the large group setting, which is much more effective than giving individual assessments to students and taking up days and even weeks. Another convenience is that the tests come with specific instructions and protocol, which allows them to be more uniformly administered. The scoring is convenient as well because the teachers don't have to spend much time in grading; the answer documents are merely collected and run through a scoring machine. This allows teachers and students to get back to their regular class routines.

STANDARD OF EXCELLENCE

The creation of the state standards has outlined an expectation of what students should know at each grade level. This information is not only available to schools and teachers, but to parents and students as well in order to clarify the criteria expected in order to be promoted to the next grade. One downfall to this is that a lack of standard in the curriculum could lead to extreme differences in the quality of education between schools, making it unfair to those required to send their children to public schools due to where they reside.

FAIRNESS OF ASSESSMENT

Because all students are held accountable to the same criteria, this makes state standardized tests a fair assessment. "If schools were allowed to assess their students according to their own standards, one school could claim overwhelming success while another showed mediocre performance, and the public would have no objective way to measure one against the other" (Cascio, 2015). The fact that everyone is held to the same standard holds up even to public scrutiny as there can be no argument that all schools were evaluated fairly in comparison with one another.

STUDENT BENEFITS

Educators can better target weaknesses when they know how a student's objective performance compares with others. Through the use of technology, the information gathered from standardized tests can be provided at low costs and utilize very little class time. In a comparative study done by Bishop (1998), it was concluded that "countries requiring students to take nationally standardized tests, showed higher scores on international tests than those countries that did not require such tests."

In a second study by Bishop (2000), it was found that "U.S. students who anticipated having to pass a standardized test for high school graduation learned more science and math, were more likely to complete homework and talk with their parents about schoolwork, and watched less television than peers who were not required to pass such exams."

One argument against standardized tests is that by only testing reading and math for student accountability, an environment of neglecting other content areas such as history, science, and economics is created and reinforced. This can be perceived, however, in a positive way as well, in that systematic testing needs to be done across content areas at all grade levels.

Another argument against testing is that do not test critical thinking or problem solving but simply information that is memorized. Although tests that assess advanced understanding and judgment do exist, "the majority of standardized tests do not require respondents to identify the best reason for an action, nor the best interpretation of a set of ideas let alone the application of important principles" (Walberg, 2012). Yet another viewpoint against tests is the fact that educators and students are placed under extreme stress. The bottom line here is that the world is a demanding place and being successful in it requires adequate knowledge and better skills. If students are to be truly successful in their lives, they will need to experience some pressure and measurement scales in which they are held accountable.

SOURCE OF PRIDE

One of the main complaints posed by testing critics involves the malaise it causes among educators. Although many good schools claim to focus on student learning, they do not mention the satisfaction of the professional staff as a priority. Advocates of standardized testing state that if the data shows that the testing benefits students, it should not matter whether teachers support it.

"Good student performance on tests should be a source of satisfaction among successful educators. The appropriate tests can reveal strengths and weaknesses in the curriculum and instruction. Our nation's poor achievement progress shows that substantial improvements in teaching and learning are needed—and progress on those two fronts can and should be measured by standardized tests" (Walberg, 2011).

Are there truly any benefits to standardized testing? It depends on which side of the playground you stand. My viewpoint is just that, mine. There are those who feel "recess" is a waste and that time should be spent studying for the test. Then there are those who believe that there is much real-world learning to be done through the interaction and socialization of "playing" with others.

Chapter 10

Are There Alternatives to Standardized Testing?

Education ceases to be learning when the 3 R's are read, remember, and regurgitate.

—Student protestor on the TV show *Boston Public*

The fact is that paper-and-pencil tests give teachers only a small part of the picture of a child's strengths and weaknesses. The most effective use of these tests is when teachers use them in combination with the results of many other variables in order to give insight into a child's true knowledge and abilities. These other variables may include:

- Informal assessments through the observation of students;
- Previewing and grading day-to-day class work;
- Homework assignments need to be graded;
- Parent conferences and meetings; and
- Tracking student progress throughout the year.

Few can argue that standardized tests have limitations. They are not a perfect measure of what a student can or cannot do nor of all they have learned. Of course, as with human nature, a student's achievement can vary from day to day on the basis of their motivation and choice of approach: guessing to answer a question, reading the question carefully, or taking the test as a serious endeavor.

According to Flanogan, Mascolo, and Hardy-Braz (2009), some alternative tests include:

1. **Curriculum-Based Assessment:** Relies on a teacher's direct observations of a student's performance in comparison with the curriculum in order to make instructional decisions (Deno, 1987, p. 41). This is

sometimes referred to as a direct assessment which measures the mastery of academic skills.

Probes are developed in each academic area (i.e., short reading passages, samples of math computation items, and brief spelling word lists) based on the curricular materials being taught which are then used in order to collect performance data.

To evaluate the probes, students are observed while reading and writing in their academic environment. During this time, data is collected and used in order to assess whether a student is progressing adequately or falling behind. These probes need to be done on a regular basis in order to effectively track student learning.

2. **Dynamic Assessment:** This involves the use of an active teaching process in order to assess learning (Lidz, 1987). This method allows an individual's cognitive functioning to be modified while also observing changes in learning and their use of problem-solving strategies. Dynamic assessment has the following primary goals:

   - Evaluate a student's ability to critically assess principles that underlay a problem in order to generate a solution
   - Assess whether the types of instruction and the amount of time spent covering a topic actually led to student understanding
   - Identify cognitive deficits and/or noncognitive factors in terms of performance failures so teaching can be modified in order to address them (Lidz, 1987).

   This model differs from the standardized assessment as it is based on a format where the examiner presents the question, records the response, and awards the response on the basis of a set rubric. There are some disadvantages to this model, which include:

   - It requires time and skill to implement this assessment approach.
   - It is unknown as to how much modifiability can occur across all the cognitive domains.
   - It is much more complex to validate this model due to its broad goals.
   - The test is administered in a nonstandard and inconsistent nature, making it difficult to replicate.

3. **Alternative or Portfolio-Based Assessment:** Pieces of a student's work showing what learning had occurred over a span of several years are selected by the student, teacher, and parent. Utilizing this approach has been shown to encourage active participation in the documentation process of a student's learning by all the relevant individuals in the child's

life (Quinto and McKenna, 1977). Some things that are generally included in the portfolio are tape-recorded samples of oral reading, results of reading interviews, and student's reading lists which help gain information on topic interests of students.

In most cases, the assessment is derived from the daily classroom work of the student. The main goal of this model is to improve both teaching methods and student learning.

Schools utilizing this model are successful because they take kids seriously and understand their needs, concerns, questions, and interests. A great classroom is inviting, filled with learning in the forms of discrete activity centers, student work is posted on the walls, and it is evident that kids are learning with and from one another. Desks are not in rows and the climate of the room radiates a feeling that the decisions in the class are made collaboratively.

Kamenetz (2015) adds the following alternatives to the list:

4. **Sampling:** This is a method in which a select number of student scores on a traditional standardized test are collected, instead of using every single student's scores, every year. "This method is not only used by the National Assessment of Educational Progress (NAEP) also known as the Nation's Report Card but also by the widely respected international test known as the PISA. Both tests are given to a different sample of students each year in grades 4, 8 and 12" (Kamenetz, 2015).
5. **Stealth Assessment:** This approach still uses data from reading and math tests, but it is unique in how the data is collected. Textbook companies sell software designed to help students practice math and English. How it differs from traditional standardized tests is that this software records every answer a child gives, which, in turn, allows educators to collect data over a period of time revealing a student's knowledge. By tracking the data over a period of time instead of just one moment as in standardized tests, a student's ability to learn and the consistency of applying the knowledge can be better determined.
6. **Multiple Measures:** This model allows schools to use information such as graduation rates, discipline outcomes, demography, and teacher-created assessments to gauge the performance of not only the students, but the schools and teachers as well, over a period of time.
7. **Game-Based Assessment:** Video game–like assessments that are geared toward higher-order thinking have flooded the education market. These can aid in the analysis of standardized testing data because they provide insight into a student's thinking and application of skills for real-world problem solving.

NONDISCRIMINATORY ASSESSMENT: SOME RECOMMENDATIONS FOR REDUCING BIAS

Regardless of the efforts most producers make to ensure their tests are low in bias, the fact is that bias-free tests do not exist. According to Whiting and Ford (2009), the following are suggestions as to how to get closer to this goal:

- For ELLs, the test can be translated into their first language.
- Depending on the needs of the students, translators can be available for examinees.
- Preview the test in order to identify biases and eliminate those items.
- Eliminate items that may not be fair to those students from various cultures or low socioeconomic backgrounds.
- Background experience plays a huge role in a child's education. This should always be considered when interpreting test scores.
- Every student comes with different backgrounds and experiences that affect their test performance. Do not ignore this fact when utilizing standardized tests.
- No one likes to be judged by one action or one outcome and one piece of information or score should never be the basis for decisions about a child's education.
- Multiple types of assessment data should be combined in order to make comprehensive decisions versus using one test score in isolation.
- Notice patterns in group data, as often times when these scores are low, it is the test that may create the problem, and elimination of the test or certain items may be needed.
- Through the tracking of data, if it is found that a group consistently has low scores, take the time to investigate possible factors and provide strategies that would be helpful for that group.
- In tests, there are also technical and social merits to be considered. It is possible for a test to be both unbiased and unfair.

As of 2004, 43 percent of the U.S. public school population was culturally diverse. The last decade has seen an enormous change in school demographics and a rapid increase in the reliance on tests for decision making. This use of high-stakes testing in order to open or close doors to the future is a concern that needs to be addressed before more damage is done. In today's schools, test results are more often than not overinterpreted or underinterpreted and given far too much power in making decisions that could cause damage to a student's personal worth and value.

Standardized tests are here to stay. The dilemma that faces policy and educational decision makers is how to reduce bias, human errors, stereotypes, and prejudice and create an accurate measurement of student learning and understanding. Currently, many districts have attempted this by increasing the number of tests without taking into consideration the lack of real-world application for students.

Chapter 11

Will the Reauthorization of the Elementary and Secondary Act Fix the Problems?

NCLB was based on the idea that the federal government's nine-percent stake in public-education funding could be leveraged to drive significant reform. But experience is showing again the limits (and potential dangers) of what Washington can do.

—Dan Lipps, 2008

In December 2015, the reauthorization of the fifty-one-year-old Elementary and Secondary Act was signed into law. According to the Senate Committee on Health, Education, Labor and Pensions (2014), this new act, named the Every Student Succeeds Act (ESSA), has the following functions (I have added the description of the law and the parts so you can better determine which parts, if any, the new law [ESSA] is addressing.):

- **Strengthens state and local control:** Working together, states and stakeholders take on the responsibility of ensuring that all students are college and career ready by creating an accountability system. Within the accountability system, there must be minimal federal criteria such as the inclusion of all subgroup students, a method for disaggregating student data, and maintaining high levels of rigor. Accountability will still be submitted to the education department and the federal government cannot determine or approve state standards. The new plans will begin in the 2017–2018 school year. It requires states to release the names of the peer reviewers to the public, and provides states with the ability to request a hearing if the Education Department turns down their plan.
- **Maintains important information for parents, teachers, and communities:** The two tests in reading and math for children in grades 3–8 will still exist as well as the science test (three times between grades 3–10)

and the one high-school assessment. These important measures of student achievement ensure that parents know how their children are performing and help teachers support students who are struggling to meet state standards. A pilot program will allow states additional flexibility to experiment with innovative assessment systems within states. ESSA ends federal accountability and requires that data needs to be disaggregated by subgroups and reported annually. Subgroups will include low-income students, students of color, special education, and ELLs. States will select their goals and must incorporate at least four indicators into their accountability system. The first three are standard ones and include proficiency on state tests, English language proficiency, and a subgroup academic factor. The fourth indicator is to be chosen by the state and could include student engagement or school climate safety, for example. The federal government will still require that 95 percent of students participate in testing and it prohibits school districts creating super subgroups by combining different sets of students to skew accountability. Up to seven states can apply to try out local tests for a limited time, with the permission of the U.S. Department of Education. Districts can use local, nationally recognized tests at the high-school level, with state permission, such as the SAT or ACT. States can create their own testing opt-out laws, and states decide what should happen in schools that miss targets.

- **Maintains important protections for federal taxpayer dollars:** Federal dollars will continue to be protected as will federal supplements to state and local education, including additional flexibility in meeting these requirements by school districts.

- **Helps states fix the lowest-performing schools:** Federal grants will still be offered to states and school districts in order to assist low-performing schools identified by the state. At least once every three years the bottom 5 percent of low-performing schools must be identified. In addition, high schools with a 67 percent or less graduation rate and schools with high percentages of struggling subgroup students will also experience state intervention.

  For the bottom 5 percent of schools and for high schools with high dropout rates: An evidence-based plan will be created with collaboration from districts, teachers, and school staff that focus on particular groups of students that fall behind. Districts will work with teachers and school staff to come up with an evidence-based plan. States will monitor the turnaround effort. If schools continue to flounder, after no more than four years, the state will be required to step in with its own plan.

  For schools where subgroups students are struggling: The district may refer to the comprehensive improvement plan provision to target chronically underperforming subgroups. Through the SIG Program an

Will the Reauthorization of the Elementary and Secondary Act Fix the Problems? 69

increase of 4 percent (totally 7 percent) in Title I funds will be set aside for school improvement.

TITLE I—IMPROVING THE ACADEMIC ACHIEVEMENT OF THE DISADVANTAGED
  PART A—IMPROVING BASIC PROGRAMS OPERATED BY LOCAL EDUCATIONAL AGENCIES
  PART B—STUDENT READING SKILLS IMPROVEMENT GRANTS
  PART C—EDUCATION OF MIGRATORY CHILDREN
  PART D—PREVENTION AND INTERVENTION PROGRAMS FOR CHILDREN AND YOUTH WHO ARE NEGLECTED, DELINQUENT, OR6.5 AT-RISK

- **Helps states support teachers:** Funds will be distributed to states and school districts so teachers, principals, and other educators can be supported through the implementation of various activities such as mentoring programs for new teachers and professional development trainings and programs for educators.

TITLE II—TEACHER QUALITY ENHANCEMENT
  PART A—TEACHER QUALITY ENHANCEMENT GRANTS FOR STATES AND PARTNERSHIPS';
  PART B—PREPARING TOMORROW'S TEACHERS TO USE TECHNOLOGY
  PART F—GENERAL EDUCATION PROVISIONS ACT
  PART G—MISCELLANEOUS OTHER STATUTES
  PART J—CERTAIN MULTIYEAR GRANTS AND CONTRACTS
TITLE II—PREPARING, TRAINING, AND RECRUITING HIGH-QUALITY TEACHERS AND PRINCIPALS
  PART A—TEACHER AND PRINCIPAL TRAINING AND RECRUITING FUND
  PART B—MATHEMATICS AND SCIENCE PARTNERSHIPS
  PART C—INNOVATION FOR TEACHER QUALITY
  PART D—ENHANCING EDUCATION THROUGH TECHNOLOGY

- **Ends federal mandates on evaluations, allows states to innovate**: One option available on ESSA is the implementation of a teacher evaluation system. The definition of a highly qualified teacher is eliminated which provides states the opportunity to set the criteria for this term.

- **Helps states support English learners:** High-quality language instruction educational programs are expensive and this law provides resources that will assist ELL and immigrant children of second-language acquisition.

States are required to measure each school district's progress in the area of language instruction and provide evidence that assistance and support was or was not effective. Incentives are offered to states to enable school districts to implement policies and practices that increase instruction of second-language learners and professional development for teachers. Entrance and exit procedures for ELL programs will be established and implemented by each state and the federal government will provide states and school districts with additional options for long-term ELLs and ELLs with disabilities. Accountability for ELLs has been moved from Title III (the English language acquisition section of the ESSA) to Title I (where everyone else's accountability is), it is believed that it forces districts to make these students a priority. For schools to include ELLs test scores, a student must reside in the United States for one year. In the first year, such students are expected to take the assessments, but their scores are not averaged into the school accountability rating. In the second year, the students' test scores may be included as a record of their measurement of growth. In the third year, the students' scores shall be recorded and included in data reports as any other child's.

TITLE III—LANGUAGE INSTRUCTION FOR LIMITED
ENGLISH-PROFICIENT AND IMMIGRANT STUDENTS
    PART A—ENGLISH LANGUAGE ACQUISITION, LANGUAGE
    ENHANCEMENT, AND ACADEMIC ACHIEVEMENT ACT
    PART B—IMPROVING LANGUAGE INSTRUCTION
    EDUCATIONAL PROGRAMS
    PART C—GENERAL PROVISIONS

- **Requires community-based needs assessments to better target funding:** A collaboration between schools, districts, parents, teachers, and all stakeholders will create a plan in order to implement various comprehensive programs targeting student safety, health, well-being, and academic achievement. A needs assessment will be included in the plan to measure school quality, climate, safety, discipline, and any other additional risk factor in order to channel funding where it is needed the most.

TITLE IV—21ST-CENTURY SCHOOLS
    PART A—SAFE AND DRUG-FREE SCHOOLS
    AND COMMUNITIES
    PART B—21ST-CENTURY COMMUNITY
    LEARNING CENTERS
    PART C—ENVIRONMENTAL TOBACCO SMOKE

- **Affirms state responsibility for supporting the coordination and implementation of high-quality programs and initiatives:** Coordination and integration of program barriers must be identified and eliminated by the state. This includes initiatives and funding streams, and technical assistance and training. The main goal here is to get best practices implemented in order to create a school climate where all students' needs are being met.

- **Updates and strengthens charter school programs:** Within the ESSA the two existing programs from NCLB will be combined to create one charter school program made up of three grant competitions:
  a. *High-Quality Charter Schools*: Grants for the development of new charter schools, to expand an already established charter school which includes the hiring and preparation of teachers and transportation of students.
  b. *Facilities Financing Assistance*: Incentives in the form of grants to be innovative in crating methods of enhancing credit to finance the acquisition, construction, or renovation of a charter school.
  c. *Replication and Expansion:* Replication can be the highest compliment. These grants are distributed to charter management organizations so that they can duplicate or expand successful charter schools.

  The law also provides incentives for states to adopt stronger charter school authorizing practices, increases charter school transparency, and improves community engagement in the implementation and operation of each charter school receiving funds to ensure charter school success.

TITLE V—PROMOTING INFORMED PARENTAL CHOICE AND INNOVATIVE PROGRAMS
    PART A—INNOVATIVE PROGRAMS
    PART B—PUBLIC CHARTER SCHOOLS
    PART C—MAGNET SCHOOLS ASSISTANCE
    PART D—FUND FOR THE IMPROVEMENT OF EDUCATION

- **Prioritizes grants to evidence-based magnet school programs:** This includes interdistrict and regional magnet programs and also provides opportunities for those magnet schools that have demonstrated a record of success to expand. The impact of activities will be monitored and evaluated for its ability to improve socioeconomic and racial integration as well as student achievement.

- **Supports rural schools:** Federal funding will be more flexible in order to support rural districts in the effective implementation of programs while also maintaining the authorization of the Small, Rural School Achievement (SRSA) program and the Rural and Low-Income School (RLIS) program. Some districts are dually eligible for both the SRSA and the RLIS and ESSA allows them to choose which program they would like to apply without penalties.

TITLE VI—FLEXIBILITY AND ACCOUNTABILITY
    PART A—IMPROVING ACADEMIC ACHIEVEMENT
    PART B—RURAL EDUCATION INITIATIVE
    PART C—GENERAL PROVISIONS

- **Supports programs for American Indian and Alaska Native students:** Competitive and formula grants are provided in order to support local development of programs for American Indian and Alaska Native students. A greater coordination between local community schools and tribes will be fostered for all Native American students.

TITLE VII—INDIAN, NATIVE HAWAIIAN, AND ALASKA NATIVE EDUCATION
    PART A—INDIAN EDUCATION
    PART B—NATIVE HAWAIIAN EDUCATION
    PART C—ALASKA NATIVE EDUCATION

- **Updates the Impact Aid formula:** The National Defense Authorization Act replaces the outdated Impact Aid formula and contains a simple, objective calculation for schools to be eligible for programs. The goal here is to remove subjectivity and speed up payments to school districts.

TITLE VIII—IMPACT AID PROGRAM

- **Improves maintenance of effort requirements:** Federal dollars must be fiscally protected and yet states must also be given the flexibility to meet maintenance of effort requirements. ESSA helps to ensure that the supplemental state and local education dollars are protected.

TITLE IX—GENERAL PROVISIONS
    PART A—DEFINITIONS
    PART B—FLEXIBILITY IN THE USE OF ADMINISTRATIVE AND OTHER FUNDS
    PART C—COORDINATION OF PROGRAMS; CONSOLIDATED STATE AND LOCAL PLANS AND APPLICATIONS
    PART D—WAIVERS
    PART E—UNIFORM PROVISIONS

- **Prohibits federal government from imposing additional requirements on states seeking waivers:** ESSA not only prohibits mandating additional requirements when states or school districts seek waivers from federal law but also limits the authority that the secretary has to reject a waiver request.

- **Ensures homeless students have access to critical supports to improve school stability:** Many unique challenges come with educating the homeless. ESSA supports these students and is committed to helping them succeed in school. District liaisons are assigned and specially trained to not only increase support for these youth but also provide resources that will increase student stability. Homeless youth will also be guaranteed access to all educational services, including charter and magnet schools, summer school, career and technical education, advanced placement, and online learning.

TITLE X—REPEALS, REDESIGNATIONS, AND AMENDMENTS TO OTHER STATUTES
    PART A—REPEALS
    PART B—REDESIGNATIONS
    PART C—HOMELESS EDUCATION
    PART D—NATIVE AMERICAN EDUCATION IMPROVEMENT
    PART E—BUREAU OF INDIAN AFFAIRS PROGRAMS

EARLY CHILDHOOD

- **Ensures that federal funds may be used for early education programs:** Early childhood education receives federal funds specifically designed for these programs' needs. The funds from Title I, Title II, and Title III are provided to improve early childhood education programs and help them to run smoothly.

The ESSA enshrines the Preschool Development Grant program in law and focuses it on program coordination, quality, and broadening access to early-childhood education. But the program is housed at the Department of Health and Human Services, jointly administered by the Education Department. A new evidence-based research and innovation program is created, described by some as similar to the Obama administration's Investing in Innovation Program. Other highlights include a standalone program for parent engagement, along with reservations for arts education, gifted and talented education, and Ready to Learn Television. (Education Week, 2015)

According to Walker (2015), many of the major elements are already improving, but educators are still voicing concerns about the implementation of new assessment and accountability systems. Their concerns are as follows:

- Multiple measures need to be used in order to evaluate student performance in the elementary and middle school levels.
- At least one indicator of student or school support should be met within a school's or district's accountability system in order to help draw attention to achievement gaps. Some suggestions include access to advanced course work, school counselors, nurse, fine arts, and regular physical education opportunities.

- Parents should be given the choice to opt out of state-designed assessments without penalty.
- Assessment systems need to be audited and the process streamlined through some type of measurement tool.
- Assessments need to be based on the combination of teaching and learning along with accountability. State-designed assessments that reflect this should be made available to all states meeting this criteria.
- A strong start in early childhood is important if students are to be successful. A grant should be created for states in order to set up early childhood systems.
- The distribution of federal teacher development funds has a new formula that ties funds to population and poverty changes in each state. How will this affect their state?

WHAT THE REWRITE DOESN'T ADDRESS

Walker (2015) admits that while these are big wins, work continues toward producing a final law that progresses in a number of key areas, including:

- Reducing the excessive testing of students.
- Selecting grade-span testing (once in elementary, middle, and high school) that has a main focus of critical thinking instead of rote memorization.
- States should be mandated to include a more comprehensive range of student support and school success indicators in their accountability systems.
- ESSA would maintain, however, a requirement that states keep data on whether all students are achieving, including low-income, minority, and foreign-born students, and those with disabilities.
- Not enough is being done to motivate low-performing schools to improve. States are also not being forced to address achievement gaps.
- ESSA is not ensuring that regardless of race, financial status, or residency, every child can attend a top-quality school.

Let's face it. ESSA is far from perfect. The testing will continue in grades 3–8 and high school just as it did for NCLB. It appears to emphasize a waste in taxpayer funds by allotting far too many federal dollars with minimal accountability to charter schools and continues to encourage merit pay for teachers. This money could be redirected on reducing classroom size and purchasing proven programs that protect the privacy of student data from leaking into the hands of third parties and vendors without parental knowledge or consent (Ravitch, 2015b).

This law will, however, bar the federal governments from using test scores as the sole measurement of teacher effectiveness, which will lessen the narrowing of curriculum and alleviate some of the test prep pressures. In other words, teachers will be able to truly practice their craft. TEACH. Another positive factor is that states will not be financially punished when parents exercise their right to opt out of testing (Ravitch, 2015b). To play off the famous Neil Armstrong quote, it is one small step—but a huge gain for educators and parents and thus, our children.

Conclusion

If more testing were the answer to the problems in our schools, testing would have solved them a long time ago.

—Bill Goodling, chair of House Education Committee

"Since 2012, the Obama administration has granted requests from forty-two states, Puerto Rico and the District of Columbia for waivers from some of the NCLB laws strictest requirements because it became clear they wouldn't be met" (Kerr, 2015).

Currently, annual tests for every child in reading and math occur in grades 3 and 8, and another in high school will continue to be the centerpiece of federal education law even with the ESSA (2015). The bottom line is high-stakes testing usage is on the rise with twenty-six states currently implementing a high-school exit exam.

Much controversy has been brewing about high-stakes testing. Those who advocate testing believe that a "no-excuse environment" will create and reinforce schools to get all students to achieve. Those against testing claim that a single test on one day of the school year should not determine whether a student is promoted and results in a narrowing of what is being taught in today's schools.

In reality, the main controversy truly revolves around how the results are used instead of the tests themselves. Instead of test scores standing alone in the decision-making, they should be combined with the student's grades and teacher evaluations in order to provide a more rounded measure of a student's abilities, knowledge, and skills. When properly used, tests can provide valuable insight into student understanding and critical thinking abilities, as well as identify those who are struggling and may need assistance. When misused they can have adverse consequences.

Recently, educational decision makers' discussions about cutting back on testing requirements have come at a time of growing concerns about the number of tests taken, the amount of instructional time, and the time to administer the tests. Some are taking a stand and forming groups in order to "opt out" and remove their children not only from the mandated tests but also from the endless number of state and district tests that are given.

While this book covers a broad range of high-stakes testing issues as part of the outdated NCLB Education Act of 2001, and the passing of ESSA (2015), I am glad to see that educators, parents, and policy makers are considering the many effects their decisions have on our future. Do we want a work force that needs four answer choices in order to make a decision, or one that can critically think through situations and come up with effective solutions?

Steps are being taken in the right direction, but right now, the question is, "Do the rewrites go far enough to fix the destruction that has been done to the American public school system?"

References

Abelmann, C. H., Elmore, R. F., Even, J., Kenyon, S. and Marshall, J. (2004). When accountability knocks, will anyone answer? In Richard F. Elmore (Ed.), *School Reform from the Inside Out*, 133–199. Cambridge, MA: Harvard Education Press.

Akadjian, D. (2015). Standardized tests in Texas; It's like using a bathroom scale to measure height. *Daily KOS*. Retrieved from: http://www.dailykos.com/story/2015/02/10/1363281/-Standardized-tests-in-Texas-It-s-like-using-a-bathroom-scale-to-measure-height.

American Federation of Teachers. (2013). AFT report shows the high cost of overtesting. Retrieved from: http://www.aft.org/news/aft-report-shows-high-cost-overtesting.

Anrig, G. (2015). Value subtracted. Retrieved from: http://www.slate.com/articles/Life/education/2015/03/gov_andrew_cuomo_and_teacher_evaluations_standardized_testScores_are_the.html.

Association of Test Publishers. (2014). "Questions About Testing in Schools." http://www.testpublishers.org/testing-in-schools.

Augustine, N. R. (2013). High marks for standardized tests. *The Washington Post*. Retrieved from: http://www.washingtonpost.com/opinions/high-marks-for-standardized-tests/2013/08/01/34947a2a-eb4f-11e2-a301-ea5a8116d211_story.html.

Ball, D. (1989). *Breaking with Experience in Learning to Teach Mathematics*. (Issue Paper 88). East Lansing, MI: National Center for Research on Teaching.

Biddle, B. J. and Berliner, D. C. (2002). A research synthesis; Unequal school funding. In the United States. *Educational Leadership*, 59(8), 48–59.

Bishop, J. H. (1998). The effect of curriculum-based external exam systems on student achievement. *Journal of Economic Education*, 29, 171–182.

Bishop, J. H. (2000). Curriculum-based external exam Systems: Do students learn more? How? *Psychology, Public Policy, and Law*, 6, 199–215.

Bowman, B. (1994). The challenge of diversity. 76, 234–238. *WilsonWeb*. July 16, 2001.

Broussard, M. (2014). Why poor schools can't win at standardized testing. *The Atlantic*. Retrieved from: http://www.theatlantic.com/education/archive/2014/07/why-poor-schools-cant-win-at-standardized-testing/374287/.

Bruno, R., Ashby, S. and Manzo, F. (2012). *Beyond the Classroom: An Analysis of a Chicago Public School Teacher's Actual Workday*. School of Labor and Employment Relations, University of Illinois at Urbana-Champaign.

Business Wire (2010). News corporation to acquire education technology company wireless generation. Retrieved from: http://www.businesswire.com/news/home/20101122006883/en/News-Corporation-Acquire-Education-Technology-Company-Wireless.

Butler, A. C. (2010). Repeated Testing Produces Superior Transfer of Learning Relative to Repeated Studying. *Journal of Experimental Psychology: Learning, Memory, and Cognition*, 36, 1118–1133.

Cameron, J. and Pierce, D. (1994). Reinforcement, Reward, and Intrinsic Motivation: A Meta-Analysis. *Review of Educational Research*, 64(3), 363–423.

Cascio, C. (2015). What are the benefits of having a state standardized test? *Global Post*. Retrieved from: http://everydaylife.globalpost.com/benefits-having-state-standardized-test-30717.html.

Center for Public Education (2005). Teacher quality and student achievement. *Research Review*. Retrieved from: http://www.centerforpubliceducation.org/MainMenu/Staffingstudents/teacher-quality-and-student-achievement-at-a-glance/teacher-Quality-and-student-achievement-research=review.html.

Chingos, M. (2012). Strength in numbers; State spending on K-12 assessment systems. *Brown Center on Education Policy at Brookings*. Retrieved from: http://www.brookings.edu/~/media/research/files/reports/2012/11/29%20cost%20of%20assessment%20chingos/11_assessment_chingos_final.pdf.

Chomsky, N. (2015). The dangers of standardized testing. *Creative by Nature*. Retrieved from: https://creativesystemsthinking.wordpress.com/2015/02/21/noam-chomsky-on-the-dangers-of-standardized-testing/.

Cizek, G. J. (2000). What do school standardized tests tell us? *Edu Guide*. Retrieved from: http://www.eduguide.org/article/what-do-school-standardized-tests-tell-us.

Clarke, M. (2015). Student testing: Teachers know best. *The Seattle Times*. Retrieved from: http://www.seattletimes.com/opinion/letters-to-the-editor/student-testing-teachers-know-best.

Clawson, L. (2012). Testing-driven education means giant corporate profits and 'pineapples don't have sleeves'. *Daily KOS Labor*. Retrieved from: http://www.dailykos.com/story/2012/04/30/1085807/-Testing-driven-education-means-giant-corporate-profits-and-pineapples-don-t-have-sleeves#.

Concordia University (2015). Do standardized tests show an accurate view of students' abilities? *Concordia Online Education*. Retrieved from: http://education.cu-portland.edu/blog/news/do-standardized-test-show-an-accurate-view-of-students-abilities/.

Darling-Hammond, L. (1999). Teacher quality and student achievement: A review of state policy evidence. Seattle: Center for the Study of Teaching and Policy. Retrieved from: http://www.centerforpubliceducation.org/Main-Menu/Staffingstudents/Teacher-quality-and-student-achievement-At-a-glance/Teacher-quality-and-student-achievement-References.html#sthash.tubfBoR7.dpuf.

Deci, E. L., Koestner, R. and Ryan, R. M. (1999). A Meta-Analytic Review of Experiments Examining the Effects of Extrinsic Rewards on Intrinsic Motivation. *Psychological Bulletin*, 125(6), 627–668.

Deno, S. L. (1987). Curriculum-Based Measurement. *Teaching Exceptional Children*, 20(1), 41-42.

Education Week (2015). The every student succeeds act, explained. Retrieved from: http://www.edweek.org/ew/articles/2015/12/07/the-every-student-succeeds-act-explained.html.

Erickson, M. (2012). Standardized testing: The monster that ate American Education. *Big Think*. Retrieved from: http://bigthink.com/think-tank/standardized-testing-the-monster-that-ate-american-education.

FairTest (National Center for Fair and Open Testing) (2008). Racial justice and standardized educational testing. Retrieved from: http://www.fairtest.org/sites/default/files/racial_justice_and_testing_12-10.pdf.

Ferguson, R. F. and Ladd, H. F. (1996). How and why money matters: An analysis of Alabama schools. In H. F. Ladd (Ed.), *Holding Schools Accountable: Performance-Based Reform in Education*, 265–298. Washington, DC: The Brookings Institution.

Figueroa, A. (2013). 8 Things you should know about corporations like pearson that make huge profits from standardized testing. Retrieved from: http://www.alternet.org/education/corporations-profit-standardized-tests.

Flanagan, D., Mascolo, J. and Hardy-Braz, S. (2009). Standardized testing. Retrieved from: http://www.education.com/reference/article/standardized-testing/.

Futterman, L. (2015). Beyond the classroom; Perspectives on the future of standardized testing. *Miami Herald*. Retrieved from: http://www.miamiherald.com/news/local/community/miami-dade/community-voices/article11386568.html.

Goe, L. (2007). The link between teacher quality and student outcomes: A research synthesis. Washington, DC: National Comprehensive Center for Teacher Quality. Retrieved from http://www.ncctq.org/publications/LinkBetweenTQandStudentOutcomes.pdf.

Goe, L. and Stickler, L. (2008). Teacher quality and student achievement: Making the most of recent research. *National Comprehensive Center for Teacher Quality*. Retrieved from: http://files.eric.ed.gov/fulltext/ED520769.pdf.

Goldhaber, D. and Brewer, D. J. (1997). Why don't schools and teachers seem to matter? Assessing the impact of unobservables on educational productivity. *The Journal of Human Resources*, 32(3), 505–523.

Goldhaber, D. (2002) "The Mystery of Good Teaching." *Education Next*. http://educationnext.org/the-mystery-of-good-teaching/.

Goldshteyn, A. (2014). What do standardized tests actually measure? *The Blotter*. Berkeley Carroll High School. Retrieved from: http://bcblotter.com/opinion/2014/02/23/what-do-standardized-tests-actually-measure/.

The Gordon Commission on the Future of Assessment in Education (2013). *A Public Policy Statement*. Washington, DC: Educational Testing Service.

Gregory, R. J. (2004). *Psychological Testing: History, Principles, and Applications*. Boston: Allyn & Bacon.

Hach, R. (2014). Why I hate standardized tests: A teacher's take on how to save public education. *SALON*. Retrieved from: http://www.salon.com/2014/09/13/

why_i_hate_standardized_tests_a_teachers_take_on_how_to_save_public_education/.

Hanushek, E. A. and Raymond, M. E. (2006). School accountability and school performance. *Federal Reserve Bank of St. Louis Regional Economic Development*, 2(1), 51.

Heppen, J., Wehmah Jones, A. M., Sawyer, K., Lewis, S., Horwitz, A., Simon, C., Uzzell, R. and Casserly, M. (2011). *Using Data to Improve Instruction in the Great City Schools: Documenting Current Practice*. American Institutes for Research and Council of the Great City Schools.

Hurst, M. (2015). Testing bias, cultural bias and language differences in assessment. Retrieved from: http://study.com/academy/lesson/testing-bias-cultural-bias-language-differences-in-assessments.html.

Intelligence. (n.d.). Retrieved from http://www.merriam-webster.com/dictionary/intelligence.

Job, J. (2012). The Pearson Monopoly. Oklahoma State University. Retrieved from: http://teacherblog.typepad.com/newteacher/2012/11/on-the-rise-of-pearson-oh-and-following-the-money.html.

Jouriles, G. (2014). Here's why we don't need standardized tests. *Education Week*. Retrieved from: http://www.edweek.org/ew/articles/2014/07/09/36jouriles.h33.html.

Kamenetz, A. (2015). What schools could use instead of standardized tests. Retrieved from: http://www.npr.org/sections/ed/2015/01/06/371659141/What-schools-could-use-instead-of-standardized-tests.

Kemmerling, C. (2005). The pros of standardized testing. *Education Reform*. Retrieved from: http://www.Educationreform.net.

Kerr, J. C. (2015). Focus on senate education bill after house narrowly passess No Child Left Behind revision. *U.S. News*. Retrieved from: http://www.usnews.com/news/politics/articles/2015/07/09/no-child-revision-barely-passes-house-goes-next-to-senate.

Kingkade, T. (2014). College textbook prices increasing faster than tuition and inflation. *Huffington Post*. Retrieved from: http://www.huffingtonpost.com/2013/01/04/college-textbook-prices-increase_n_2409153.html.

Kohn, A. (2000). The case against standardized testing: Raising the scores, ruining the Schools. *Center for American Progress*. Retrieved from: http://www.teacherrenewal.Wiki.westga.edu/file/view/testing,%20testing,%20testing.pdf.

Koretz, D. (2008). *Measuring Up: What Educational Testing Really Tells Us*. Cambridge, MA: Harvard University Press.

Lazarin, M. (2014). Testing overload in America's schools. *Center for American Progress*. Retrieved from: https://www.americanprogress.org/issues/education/report/2014/10/16/99073/testing-overload-in-americas-schools/.

Lidz, C. S. (1987). *Dynamic Assessment*. New York: Guilford.

Masson, M. E. and McDaniel, M. A. (1981). The Role of Organizational Processes in Longterm Retention. *Journal of Experimental Psychology: Human Learning and Memory*, 2, 100–110.

Matthews, S. (2015). Standardized testing divides us, let's unite. *Delaware Online*. Retrieved from: http://www.delawareonline.com/story/opinion/contributors/2015/03/15/standardized-testing-divides-us-unite/24807011/.

McDaniel, M. (2014). The Tyranny of Testing Part II. *Stately McDaniel Manor*. Retrieved from: https://statelymcdanielmanor.wordpress.com/2014/05/18/the-tyranny-of-testing-part-ii/.

McDermott, K. B. and Arnold, K. M. (2010). Test taking facilitates future learning. Paper presented at the meeting of the Psychonomic Society, St. Louis, MO.

Miller, G. E. (2015). What is the U.S. poverty line and could you live below it? *20 Something Finance*. Retrieved from: http://20somethingfinance.com/what-is-the-united-states-poverty-line/.

Miner, V. (2005). Keeping public schools public; Testing companies mine for Gold. *Rethinking Schools*. Retrieved from: http://www.rethinkingschools.org/Special_reports/bushplan/test192.shtml.

National Council on Teacher Quality (2014). *2013 State Teacher Policy Yearbook*. Retrieved From: http://www.nctq.org/dmsView/2013_State_Teacher_Policy_Yearbook_National_Summary_NCTQ_Report.

National Research Council (2011). Incentives and test-based accountability in education. Retrieved from: http://standardizedtests.procon.org/sourcefiles/incentives-and-test-based-accountability-in-education.pdf.

Nelson, H. (2013). Testing more, teaching less. What America's obsession with student testing costs in money and lost instructional time. *American Federation of Teachers*. Retrieved from: http://www.aft.org/sites/default/files/news/testingmore2013.pdf.

Northington, A. (2008). Poverty can adversely impact test scores. *Shreveport Times*. Retrieved from: http://archive.shreveporttimes.com/article/20080518/NEWS04/108040007/Poverty-can-adversely-impact-test-scores.

Ogbu, J. (1992). Understanding Cultural Diversity and Learning. *Educational Researcher, 21*(8), 5–14.

Persson, J. (2015). Pearson, ETS, Houghton Mifflin, and McGraw-Hill Lobby Big and Profit Bigger from School Tests. Retrieved from: http://www.prwatch.org/news/2015/03/12777/reporters-guide-how-pearson-ets-houghton-mifflin-and-mcgraw-hill-are-profiting.

Piette, B. (2014). For-profit tech corporations gain from common core testing. *Workers World*. Retrieved from: http://www.workers.org/articles/2014/06/17/profit-tech-corporations-gain-common-core-testing/.

Pollard, J. (2002). Measuring what matters least. World Prosperity Ltd. Retrieved from: http://www.standardizedtesting.net/.

ProCon (2015). Is the use of standardized tests improving education in America? Retrieved from: http://standardizedtests.procon.org.

Project Appleseed (2014). What should parents know about standardized testing? Retrieved from: http://www.projectappleseed.org/#!standardtest/c1tag.

Quinto, F. and McKenna, B. (1977). *Alternatives to Standardized Testing*. Washington, DC: National Education Association, Division of Instruction and Professional Development.

Ravitch, D. (2015a). Teachers in Washington State speak out against common core testing. *Diane Ravitch's Blog*. Retrieved from: http://dianeravitch.net/2015/03/26/teachers-in-washington-state-speak-out-against-common-core-testing/.

Ravitch, D. (2015b). Leonie Haimson; Setting the record straight about Every Child Achieves Act. *Diane Ravitch's Blog*. Retrieved from: http://dianeravitch.

net/2015/07/07/leonie-haimson-setting-the-record-straight-about-the-every-child-achieves-act/.

Reynolds, C. R. (1998). Cultural bias in testing of intelligence and personality. In A. Bellack and M. Hersen (Series Eds.) and C. Belar (Vol. Ed.), *Comprehensive Clinical Psychology: Sociocultural and Individual Differences*. New York: Elsevier Science.

Rivkin, S. G., Hanushek, E. A. and Kain, J. F. (2005). Teachers, schools and academic achievement. *Econometrica, 73*(2), 417–458.

Roediger, H. L., Putnam, A. L. and Smith, M. A. (2011). Ten Benefits of Testing and Their Applications to Educational Practice. *Psychology of Learning and Motivation*, 55. Retrieved from: http://psych.wustl.edu/memory/Roddy%20article%20PDF's/BC_Roediger%20et%20al%20(2011)_PLM.pdf.

Seaborn, J. (2015). Standardized testing and the worries it creates. *Statesman*. Retrieved from: http://viewpoints.blog.statesman.com/2015/03/05/standardized-testing-and-the-worries-it-creates/.

The Senate Committee on Health, Education, Labor and Pensions (2014). *The Every Child Succeeds Act of 2015*. Retrieved from: https://www.nsba.org/sites/default/files/file/April_2015_Senate_Every_child_Achieves_Act.pdf.

Simon, S. (2015). No Profit Left Behind: In the high stakes world of American education, Pearson makes money even when results don't measure up. *Politico Pro*. Retrieved from: http://www.politico.com/story/2015/02/pearson-education-115026.html.

Singer, A. (2013). Pearson rakes in profit (Update). *Huff Post Business*. Retrieved from: http://www.huffingtonpost.com/alan-singer/pearson-education-profits_b_2902642.html.

Son, L. K. and Kornell, N. (2008). Research on the allocation of study time: Key studies from 1890 to the present (and beyond). In J. Dunlosky, and R. A. Bjork, (Eds.), *A Handbook of Memory and Metamemory*, 333–351. Hillsdale, NJ: Psychology Press.

Spencer, K. (2013). The Pearson Monopoly. *The State Times*. Retrieved from: http://thestatetimes.com/2013/11/20/the-pearson-monopoly/.

Strauss, V. (2015). How is this fair? Art teacher is evaluated by students' math standardized test scores. *The Washington Post*. Retrieved from: http://www.washingtonpost.com/blogs/answer-sheet/wp/2015/03/25/how-is-this-fair-art-teacher-is-evaluated-by-students-math-standardized-test-scores/.

Strauss, V. (2014). Weingarten slams teacher evaluation by student test scores. *The Washington Post*. Retrieved from: http://www.washingtonpost.com/blogs/answer-sheet/wp/2014/01/13/weingarten-slams-teacher-evaluation-by-student-test-scores/.

Strauss, V. (2013). How much time do school districts spend on standardized testing? This much. *The Washington Post*. Retrieved from: http://www.washingtonpost.com/blogs/answer-sheet/wp/2013/07/25/how-much-time-do-school-districts-spend-on-standardized-testing-this-much/.

Strauss, V. (2012a). How standardized tests are affecting public schools. *The Washington Post*. Retrieved from: http://www.washingtonpost.com/blogs/answer-sheet/Post/how-standardized-tests-are-affecting-public-schools/2012/05/17/gIQABH1NXU_blog.html.

Strauss, V. (2012b). Enough with 'no excuses' rhetoric; Poverty does matter. *The Washington Post*. Retrieved from: https://www.washingtonpost.com/blogs/answer-sheet/post/the-bottom-line-on-no-excuses-and-poverty-in-school-reform/2012/09/29/813683bc-08c1-11e2-afff-d6c7f20a83bf_blog.html.

Supovitz, J. (2015). Is high-stakes testing working? Penn Graduate School of Education. Retrieved from: https://gse.upenn.edu/review/feature/supovitz.

Tennessee State Department of Education. (1985–1990). The State of Tennessee's Student/Teacher Achievement Ratio (STAR) Project. Retrieved from: http://d64.e2services.net/class/STARsummary.pdf.

Texas Classroom Teachers Association (2014). The prevalence of poverty. *The Classroom Teacher* 34(1).

University of South Florida (2002). Education policy analysis archives.10/37. College of Education Publications. Retrieved from: http://scholarcommons.usf.edu/cgi/Viewcontent.cgi?article=13988context=coedu_pub8sei-redir=18referer.

Wai, J. (2014). What do standardized tests really measure? *The Creativity Post*. Retrieved from: http://www.creativitypost.com/education/what_do_standardized_tests_really_measure.

Walberg, H. J. *Tests, Testing, and Genuine School Reform*. Washington, DC: Hoover Institution Press, 2011.

Walker, T. (2015). Educators put their stamp on NCLB rewrite. *NEA Today*. Retrieved from: http://neatoday.org/2015/04/16/educators-put-their-stamp-on-nclb-rewrite/.

Weiss, J. (2012). Texas' standardized tests a poor measure of what students learned, UT-Austin Professor says. *The Dallas Morning News*. Retrieved from: http://www.dallasnews.com/news/education/headlines/20120811-texas-standardized-tests-a-poor-measure-of-what-students-learned-ut-austin-professor-says.ece.

Whiting, G. and Ford, D. (2009). Cultural bias in testing. Retrieved from: http://www.education.com/reference/article/cultural-bias-in-testing/.

About the Author

Dr. Michele M. Wages is an assistant professor at Southeastern Oklahoma State University teaching Emergent and Developing Literacy and Diagnosis and Remediation of Reading at Elementary Level to elementary education majors. In her twenty-six-year career, she has served as an instructional specialist on title one campuses in the Dallas-Fort Worth area for nine years, including a bilingual campus with an 86 percent Hispanic student enrollment and a free and reduced lunch demographic of 96 percent. She has also served as a classroom teacher, reading specialist, and language arts facilitator and has provided staff development training for teachers in Texas.

Dr. Wages received her bachelor's degree in social science and elementary education from the University of Michigan in Flint, her master's in educational leadership from Texas Wesleyan University located in Fort Worth, Texas, and her doctorate degree in curriculum and instruction from Capella University in Minneapolis, Minnesota. Her dissertation topic dealt with the effects of two types of bilingual programs on Hispanic student achievement in reading for grades 3–6. She has also authored the following titles:

- *Engaging the Hispanic Learner: 10 Strategies in Using Culture to Increase Student Achievement*
- *Creating Culturally Responsive Schools: One Classroom at a Time*
- *Culture, Poverty and Education: What's Happening in Today's Schools?*
- *Parent Involvement: Collaboration Is the Key for Every Child's Success*

Michele currently resides in Fort Worth, Texas, and travels to many states as a consultant and trainer of how to better address the increasing diversity in today's public schools.

www.ingramcontent.com/pod-product-compliance
Lightning Source LLC
Chambersburg PA
CBHW030147240426
43672CB00005B/308